Adobe Illustrator
A Visual Guide for the Mac

*A step-by-step approach
to learning illustration software*

Janet Ashford and Linnea Dayton

Addison-Wesley Publishing Company

Reading, Massachusetts • Menlo Park, California • New York
Don Mills, Ontario • Wokingham, England • Amsterdam
Bonn • Sydney • Singapore • Tokyo • Madrid • San Juan
Paris • Seoul • Milan • Mexico City • Taipei

Library of Congress Cataloging-in-Publication Data has been applied for.

ISBN 0-201-40723-X

Cover design by Janet Ashford
Book design by Janet Ashford and Linnea Dayton
Set in Garamond Light Condensed and Franklin Gothic Condensed
by Janet Ashford and Linnea Dayton
Imagesetting by Laser Express of San Diego, California

Manufactured in Hong Kong
First printing, February 1995

Addison-Wesley books are available for bulk purchases by corporations, institutions, and other organizations. For more information about how to make such purchases in the United States, please contact the Corporate, Government, and Special Sales Department at 1-800-238-9682.

Dedication

To John Odam, for many years of encouragement and support
J.A.

In memory of David Smith, fine artist and pioneer of PostScript illustration
L.D.

Acknowledgments

We would like to thank all the artists and designers whose work appears in this book. They generously shared their time and computer files and we enjoyed working with them.

We would also like to thank our imagesetting service bureaus, Laser Express in San Diego, California and Adage Graphics in Los Angeles, California for their dedication to the job of producing film from our electronic files. Special thanks go to Doug Isaacs, Janet's brother, for sharing his expertise in electronic pre-press. In electronic publishing endeavors, it's important to have the support of output professionals who understand your goals and will work with you to achieve them.

Both of us are fortunate to be able to work at home, and so this book came together amid the support and welcome distractions provided by our families and friends.

In addition to being professional colleagues and co-authors, we are also friends and neighbors, so we would like to thank each other. It is a treasure to be able to work with a friend.

Janet Ashford and Linnea Dayton

Contents

Creating Illustrations

Designing Publications

Production

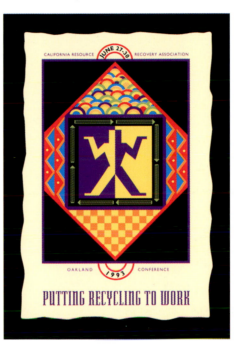

How To Use This Book

In this book the pictures and their captions tell the story. Here are some tips that will help you find the kinds of information you need.

- Graphics Techniques
- Creating Logos and Identities
- Creating Illustrations
- Designing Publications
- Production

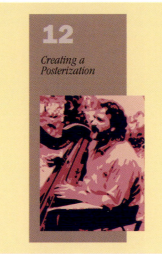

12

Creating a Posterization

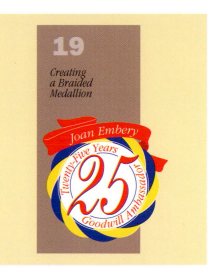

19

Creating a Braided Medallion

Covering the subject

This book shows, step-by-step, how to use Adobe Illustrator on a Macintosh computer. Chapter 1 briefly reviews program basics, covering the page layout topics shown here. It also includes keyboard shortcuts and tips for using the software easily and efficiently.

Presenting specific techniques

The subsequent chapters are of 2 types. In some chapters we have put together demonstrations of techniques that we think all users of Adobe Illustrator will want to know about. ⬤ *This apple symbol signals useful tips and shortcuts.*

Describing real-world projects

Other chapters tell how illustrators and designers have used Illustrator to produce a wide variety of artwork. The finished work is shown in the title block of the chapter, along with the designer's name.

Creating Logos and Identities

Working in layers

Adobe Illustrator artwork is assembled in layers. So the descriptions of many of the projects in the book are presented according to "layering logic," working from background to foreground. The artists themselves often used a freer, more experimental process.

Finding information

The projects and techniques are grouped within sections of the book according to the topics listed in "Covering the subject," above. To find a project by topic, check the table of contents. Most projects involve more than 1 technique and could have been placed in any of the several sections of the book. The index in the back of the book will help you find references to specific techniques — for example, the use of particular drawing tools and filters.

Browsing

Because the book is so highly visual, one way to locate a specific technique — or just to find inspiration or a jumping-off point for your own exploration — is to flip the pages of the book and look at the pictures. We hope you will enjoy the book and find it useful.

1

The Illustrator Basics

Janet Ashford

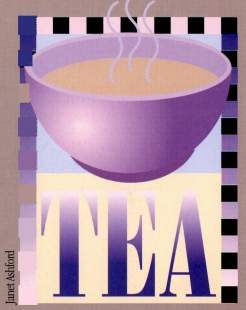

This chapter presents some basic information about using Illustrator's basic functions for drawing shapes and lines, transforming objects, copying and pasting, using color and gradients, creating blends, working with type, and graphing.

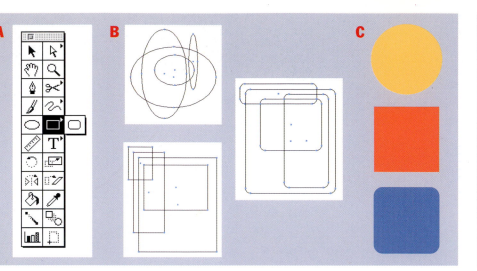

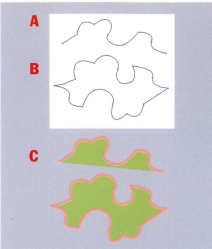

1 Drawing geometric shapes

Adobe Illustrator's drawing tools (A) — the geometric tools (oval, rectangle, and rounded rectangle), the pen, the brush, and the freehand tool — provide a range of drawing capabilities. Preformed ovals, rectangles, and rectangles with rounded corners can be drawn from an edge to any size and proportions by dragging the tool diagonally (B). Double-clicking a geometric tool in the toolbox or holding down the Option key while drawing makes the tool draw outward from the center of the shape. Holding down the Shift key constrains the shapes to 1:1 proportions, producing circles or squares (C).

2 Drawing paths with the pen tool

The pen tool is used to draw paths by placing Bezier anchor points 1 at a time. Paths can be left open (A) or can be closed by clicking on the starting point again (B). Both kinds of paths can be given a stroke and fill (C).

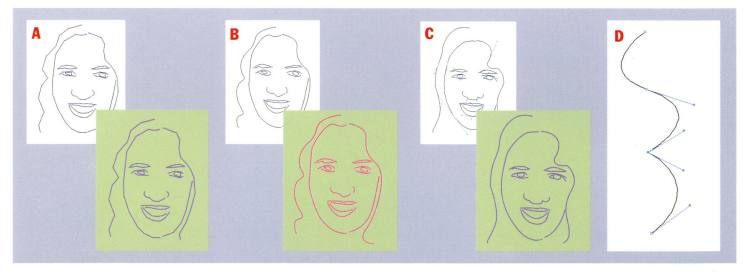

3 Drawing smooth and corner points

Clicking from point to point with the pen tool creates straight lines connected by corner points (A). To draw curves with smooth points, hold down the mouse button to place the point and then drag to form a direction line tangent to the anchor point with a direction point at each end. The length and slope of the direction line determine the height and slope of the curve (B). To draw a path with both corner and smooth points, combine mouse clicks and hold-and-drag movements (C). To draw 2 curves with a corner point in between, draw a curve and then hold down the Option key, click on the last anchor point, and drag to form a new direction line; then release the Option key and mouse, place a new anchor where the next curve should end, and drag to define it. The corner point's 2 direction lines can be moved independently (D). ⌘ *To edit a curve, hold down the Command key while the pen tool is selected and use the pointer to drag 1 of the direction points of a selected anchor point.*

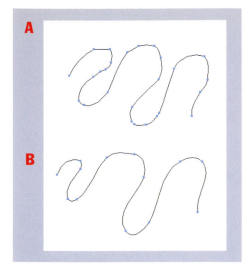

4 Drawing freehand

The freehand tool places anchor points automatically as you draw. By changing the General Preferences setting for Freehand Tolerance you can make the curve more detailed (with lower settings) (A) or smoother (with higher settings) (B).

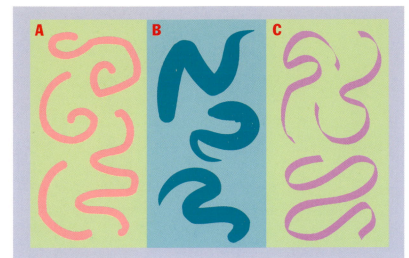

5 Creating brushstrokes

The brush tool can be used for painterly or calligraphic strokes. Instead of making a single point-by-point open path, it draws a stroke as an enclosed shape (A). For a thick-and-thin stroke, select the Variable box in the Brush dialog box and use a pressure-sensitive tablet and stylus; increasing pressure on the stylus widens the stroke (B). Select the Calligraphic box to make the brush tool operate like a calligraphic pen (C). (For more about the brush tool, see Chapter 11.)

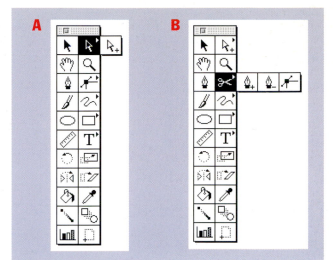

6 Finding editing tools

Illustrator provides editing tools for altering the lines and shapes made with the drawing or autotracing tools. One of these (the direct-selection arrow) is found in the top right corner of the tool palette (A). Others (scissors, add-anchor-point, delete-anchor-point, and convert-direction-point) are available in a pop-out palette from the scissors tool (B).

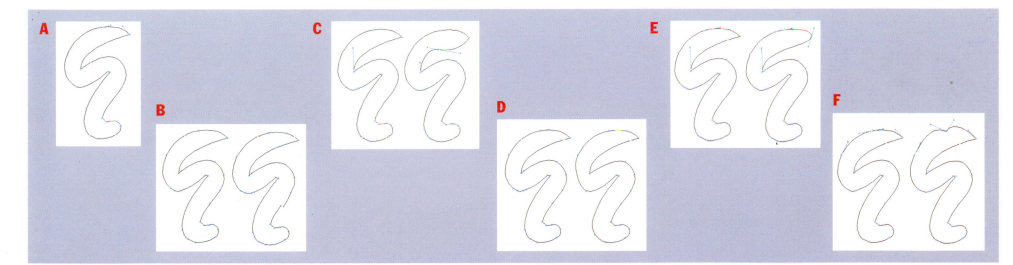

7 Editing shapes

The direct-selection tool allows you to select and move an anchor point, a line segment, or a direction point independently (A). The scissors tool breaks a line when you click it on a curve or an anchor point, creating an end point for each of the 2 sides of the split; these new points are directly on top of each other (B).

🍎 *To select the bottom anchor point after a cut has been made and dese-lected, drag the direct selection tool across the stacked points to select both points, and then Shift-click the top point to deselect it, leaving only the bottom point selected.* The add- and delete-anchor-point tools do exactly what their names suggest. Adding an anchor point allows you to increase detail by reshaping a curve (C). Removing an unnecessary point decreases the complexity of the file (D). The convert-direction-point tool will convert a smooth point into a corner point or vice versa. Clicking the tool on a corner point within a selected curve and then dragging to create the direction lines converts the point to a smooth point (E). Clicking the tool on a smooth point that has been selected with the direct-selection tool converts it to a corner point with no direction lines. To convert from a smooth point to a corner point with direction lines, click the selected point and drag to create direction lines (F).

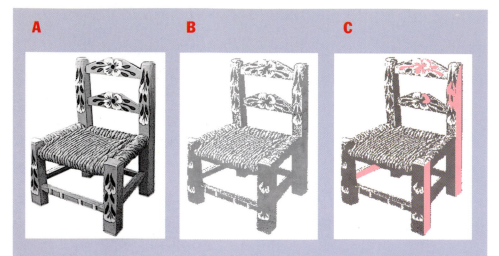

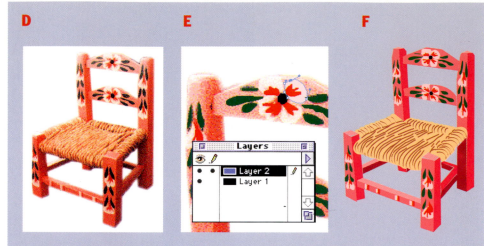

8 Tracing artwork

To trace a PICT object, you can open the PICT file (we started with a grayscale scan of a color photo) (A) as a visible but nonprinting Template in Illustrator (B) and then use either the drawing tools or the autotrace tool (a pop-out from the freehand tool) to outline its parts (C). In general, autotracing works best for simple shapes, while intricate shapes are best traced with the pen or the freehand tool. When the tracing is complete, you can delete or hide the Template.

If you'll be tracing by hand, the grayed-out Template may be difficult to trace accurately. An alternative is to trace EPS art instead of a PICT: Import an EPS file into Illustrator using the Place Art command (for this figure we used an EPS made from a color scan) (D). Then lock this imported art by clicking off the pencil icon for its layer in the Layers palette and view it in Preview mode by turning on the eye icon in the Layers palette. In a new layer, with pencil and eye showing, you can trace the imported artwork (E). Then delete the imported artwork (F).

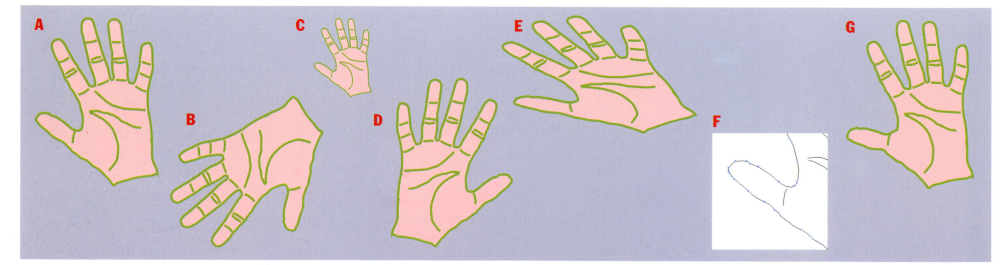

9 Transforming objects

Once you've drawn or traced an object in Illustrator (A), the transformation tools let you rotate (B), scale (C), reflect (D), or shear it (E). The object, or group of objects, must first be selected, and then the appropriate transformation tool is applied. In general, the transformation happens around the geometric center of the object unless you click to specify a different transforma-

tion center. To apply a transformation tool by hand, click once with the tool to set the point around which the transformation will occur — the point that will remain anchored in place as the transformation happens around it — and then drag from some position on or outside the object to make the transformation occur. Each transformation tool also has a dialog box, which opens if you double-click the tool in the tool palette or Option-click with the

tool instead of just clicking to define the center of the transformation; the dialog box lets you precisely specify how the transformation will occur. In some cases, you may want to transform only part of an object. Drag the direct-selection tool around the part or parts you want to change (in this case, the thumb) (F), and then apply the transformation tool. We rotated the thumb outward, leaving the rest of the hand unaltered (G).

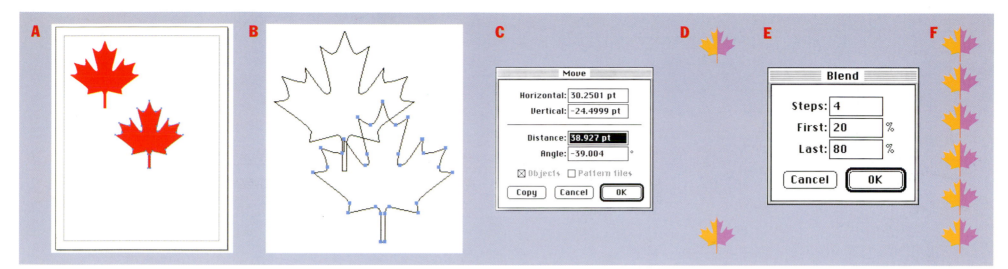

10 Copying

There are several ways to make copies of drawn or imported objects in Illustrator. One way is to select an object, choose Copy, and then choose Paste. This puts a copy of the object in the center of the screen (A). Another way is to select the object, hold down the Option key, and drag the copy to the position you choose (B). The Paste In Front and Paste In Back commands duplicate the object exactly in front of or behind the selected original; in either case the copy, not the original, is the object that remains selected after the pasting operation. An object can also be copied as it's being transformed. The dialog boxes for the rotate, reflect, shear, and scale tools include a Copy option that leaves the original object in place and creates a copy as specified in the dialog box. The Move command also includes a Copy option (C). The blend tool can be used on an object and an identical copy of that object (D) to make a number of copies — the number is set in the Blend dialog box (E) — and distribute them evenly between the 2 starting objects (F).

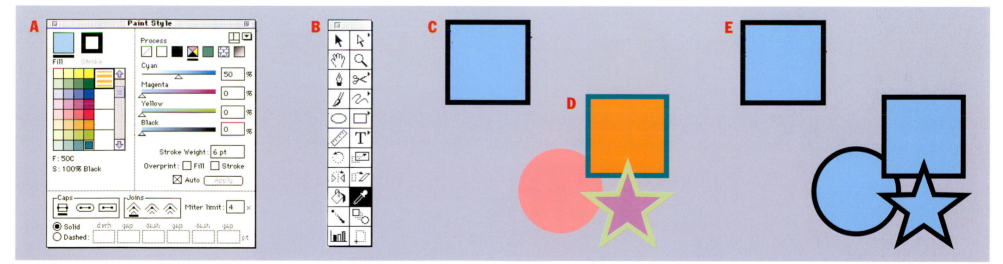

11 Applying color

Strokes (outlines) and fills can be applied to objects through the Paint Style palette (A). Strokes can be specified in terms of color, line weight, type of end cap, and dash pattern. Fills can be process colors mixed from percentages of cyan, magenta, yellow, and black; custom colors chosen from the Pantone or other color system libraries; tints of custom colors; patterns; or gradients. Both strokes and fills can be specified to overprint. The paint bucket and eyedropper tools can also be used to apply stroke and fill characteristics (B). To assign an object's stroke and fill characteristics as the current settings in the Paint Style palette, click the object with the eyedropper tool. To apply the current Paint Style settings to an object, select the object and click it with the paint bucket tool. To apply an object's stroke and fill characteristics (in this case, a blue fill and black stroke) (C) to several other objects (D), select all of the objects to be changed and then double-click on the color-source object with the eyedropper (E).

 Toggle with the Option key to select the eyedropper or paintbucket from the toolbox. Double-click the paintbucket or eyedropper tool in the toolbox to open the Paintbucket/Eyedropper dialog box to control which characteristics are picked up or applied when either tool is used.

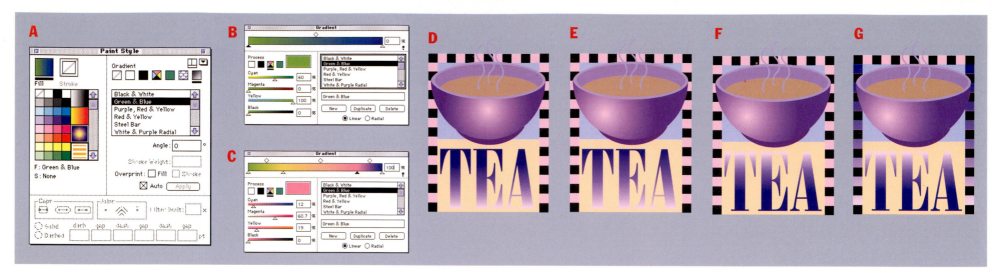

12 Using gradient fills

The uses of blends and gradient fills overlap somewhat. For many applications, the color-change effect that's needed in order to show highlighting or shading, for example, can be achieved with a gradient fill. Select the object to be filled and choose the gradient icon from the row of icons at the top of the right half of the Paint Style palette (A). Then choose a gradient from the list that appears below the icons; or double-click on a gradient name from the list, or on the gradient tool, to open the Gradient palette so you can create a new gradient to be added to the palette (B). Gradients are set up by specifying starting and ending colors and the gradient type (Linear or Radial) in the Gradient palette. More color changes can be added to the gradient by clicking below the gradient bar to add each new color change point and then selecting a color for that point (C). Once objects have been filled with linear or radial gradients (D), you can drag the gradient tool across the filled shapes to change the center of a radial fill (E) or to shift the starting or ending point of a linear fill (as in the lettering) (F) or to spread a single gradient fill over several objects (as in the colored border squares) (G).

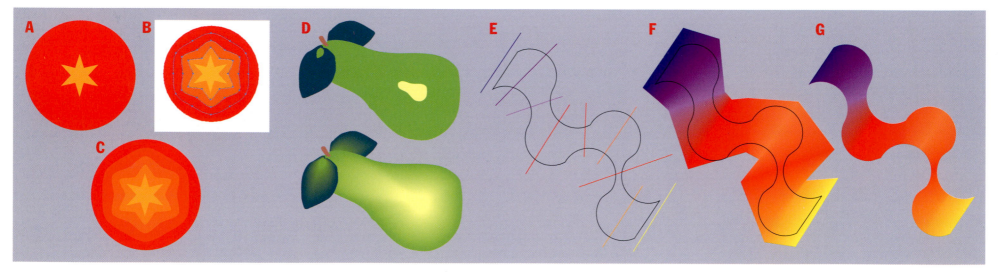

13 Using blends

The blend tool creates a series of intermediate steps between 2 lines or shapes. The resulting blend is composed of 3 objects: the 2 objects that you started with (A) and a third, grouped object that includes all the intermediate steps (B). If you don't like the result of a blend (C), it's easy to select the intermediate object, delete it, and blend again with different specifications in the Blend dialog box. When 1 line or shape is drawn on top of another and many steps are specified, the result can be a shading effect that conforms to the shapes of the objects rather than the perfectly linear or round result you get with a gradient fill (D). Blends can be masked inside of other shapes. A many-step blend of thick lines creates the same effect as a linear gradient, because the lines overlap and lose their identity as lines. Masking the blend inside a shape creates the same effect as a gradient fill. In general, using a gradient fill is easier and results in a less complex file than using such a blend. But in some cases, a blend is the only way to accomplish the desired result. For example, to create a multicolor gradient along a curved path, you can draw several lines perpendicular to a curve that bisects the shape (E); then make a series of blends, from line to line (F), and mask the blends into the shape (G).

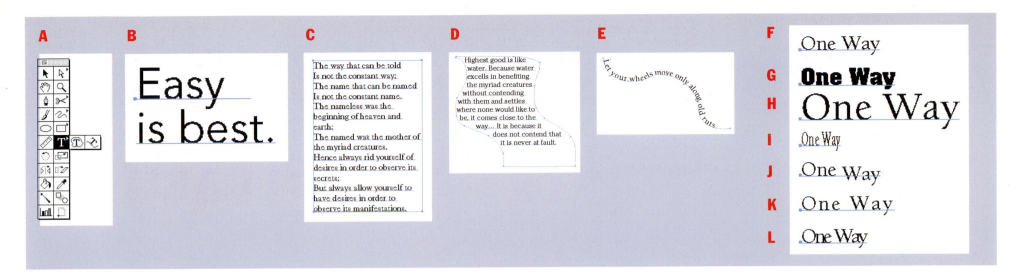

14 Using type

The type tool is used to create point type (type that is not associated with a path) and type in a rectangle. The type tool also includes 2 variations: the area-type tool is used to set type inside a path, and the path-type tool is used to set type along a path. The type tool pops out from the toolbox to show the 3 variations (A). To create point type, select the type tool, position the I-beam cursor, and begin typing (B). To create rectangle type, drag the I-beam to define a rectangle and begin typing (C). To create type inside a shape, draw and select a path, click on it with the area-type tool icon, and begin typing (D). To set type on a curve, draw and select a path, click on it with the path-type tool, and begin typing (E). Type for short headlines or logos can be entered by typing directly in Illustrator. Type for longer blocks of text can be imported from a word processor. By using the commands under the Type menu (or the Character and Paragraph palettes) you can specify many type attributes. Starting with a simple phrase (F), we changed the font (G), changed the type size (H), changed the horizontal scale (in this case we decreased it to 50%) (I), applied a baseline shift of -4 points (J), spread the type with a tracking value of 100 (K) and tightened it with a value of −100 (L).

It's also possible to specify leading, indentation, and word- and letterspacing. The Alignment command makes it possible to style paragraphs so that the text is aligned to the left margin (M) or the right margin (N), or is centered (O) or justified (P). The Rows & Columns filter, found under Text in the Filter menu, makes it possible to quickly divide a single column of rectangle type (Q) into the number of rows and columns that you specify in the Columns dialog box. We specified 2 rows, 1 column (R), 1 row, 3 columns (S), and 3 rows, 3 columns (T). Other Text filters allow you to check spelling, edit punctuation, change the case of text, and create a list of all the fonts in a document. The fill and stroke color of type can be changed using the Paint Style dialog box. Attributes can be set when the type is created and changed at any time afterward (U).

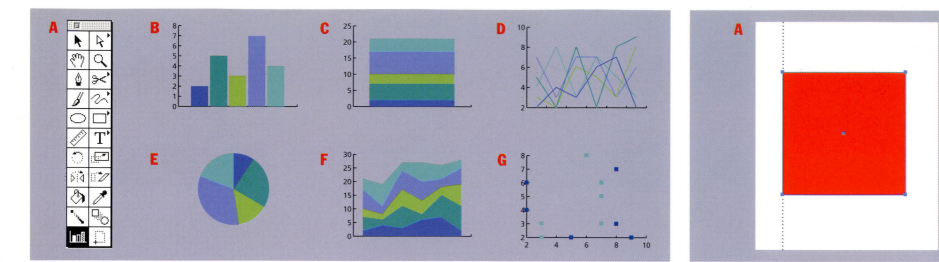

15 Graphing

Illustrator can generate graphs automatically from data you enter in a spreadsheet format. The graph style can be easily specified by selecting the graph, double-clicking on the graph tool (A), and choosing either Grouped Column (B), Stacked Column (C), Line (D), Pie (E), Area (F), or Scatter (G) from the Graph Style dialog box. After a graph is produced, it can be changed in style or modified in other ways. For example, the line weights used for axes or the type used for labels can be changed, and the strokes and fills of the bars can be altered. Illustrator constructs graphs as groups, that will change automatically when changes are made in the spreadsheet. If you want to alter type, strokes, or fills in a graph, do not ungroup it, but use the direct selection tool to select the elements you want to change.

16 Controlling the positions of objects

Illustrator provides a number of ways to precisely control the positions of elements in an illustration. When Snap To Point is selected in the General Preferences dialog box, objects moved near a nonprinting guide snap into place along the guide (A).

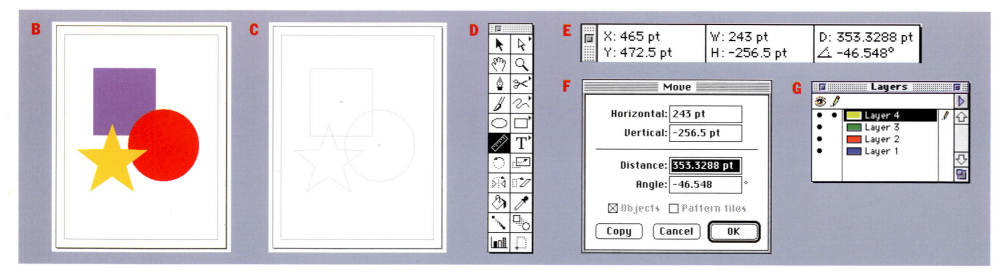

Drawn objects (B) can be turned into nonprinting guidelines by choosing Guide, Make from the Object menu. Guides appear on-screen as dotted lines (C). Guides can also be created by dragging from the rulers that appear at the right and bottom edges of the Illustrator window. ● *To lock all guides into place, choose Guide, Lock from the Object menu. To lock a single guideline, select it and choose Lock from the Arrange menu.*

The measure tool (D) lets you find the distance and angle between 2 points. The Info palette, opened by choosing Show Info from the Window menu, displays the distance and angle measured by clicking or dragging the measure tool (E). These values are also displayed in the Move dialog box (F), so that if the Move command is used immediately afterward, the selected object will be moved by the measured amounts. Any object can be selected and locked by choosing Lock from the Arrange menu. Layers of objects can also be locked, by turning off pencil icons in the Layers palette (as for layers 1, 2, and 3 shown here) (G). The Group function binds individual objects together, so the parts can't be nudged out of position. The group selection tool can be used to select groups, even those grouped within larger groups, and the direct selection tool can select a single path segment or point within a group.

2

Creating Three-Dimensional Buttons

Buttons are used in illustrations of machines and also to help guide users through interactive multimedia presentations. They are more attractive and easier to identify if they look 3-dimensional. Here are 4 styles: 2 variations of a flat raised button, a concave button, and a convex button. Our thanks to John McWade for his button ideas.

1 Creating an arrow
To create an arrow-shaped button with a simple beveled edge, first use the pen tool to draw an arrow, or type an arrow from a symbol font like Zapf Dingbats and choose Create Outlines to convert it to an outlined shape. Fill the arrow with a solid, medium-toned color like red.

2 Copying the arrow
Select and copy the red arrow and then chose Paste In Front to paste a copy exactly on top of the original. Use the Paint Style palette to apply a thick black stroke and no fill to the copy.

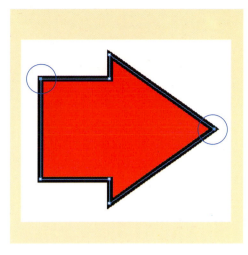

3 Splitting the copy
Use the direct selection tool to select each of the anchor points that are circled above. Click on each point with the scissors tool to split the closed path into 2 separate paths.

4 Making the end caps round
Use the Paint Style palette to specify round end caps for the 2 black lines.

5 Coloring the top edge light
Select the top line segment and change its stroke color to a lighter shade of red.

6 Coloring the bottom edge dark
Select the bottom line segment and change its stroke color to a darker shade of red. The use of round end caps and 2 colors simulates the look of a mitered corner.

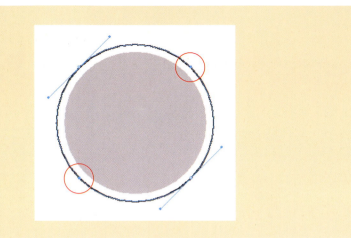

7 Drawing 2 circles

To draw a simple, raised button, first use the centered-oval tool to draw 2 concentric circles, the larger circle in back; while drawing hold down the Shift key to constrain each oval to a perfect circle. Fill the inner circle with a medium tone. Rotate the outer circle 45 degrees, select the diagonal points that are indicated, and use the scissors tool to split the circle into 2 halves. Once the outer circle has been split, the 2 end points of each half circle will automatically be connected when the path is selected and filled.

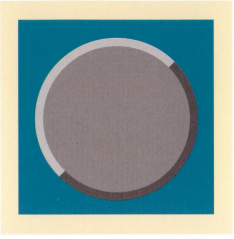

8 Filling the half circles

Fill the upper half-circle with light gray and fill the lower half-circle with dark gray. This simulates the look of a light shining across a flat button from the upper left.

9 Typing a numeral

Use the type tool to type a numeral and fill it with a tone darker than that of the face of the button.

10 Creating a highlight

Select the numeral, copy it to the clipboard, and then choose Paste In Front to paste a copy exactly on top of the original. Fill it with a lighter shade of gray and then use the Move command or the arrow keys to offset it a few points up and to the left of the original.

11 Sending the highlight behind

To send the lighter numeral backward 1 step so that it's behind the original numeral but in front of the circles, select it, choose Cut to cut it to the clipboard, select the original numeral, and choose Paste In Back to paste the lighter number in back of it, making a highlighted edge.

12 Creating a shadow

Apply the Copy and Paste in Front procedure to the original numeral again, color the copy dark gray, and move it a few points down and to the right of the original.

13 Sending the shadow behind

Cut the shadow to the clipboard, select the original numeral and choose Paste In Back to paste the shadow behind the original numeral. The shadow and highlight make the numeral look raised and 3-dimensional.

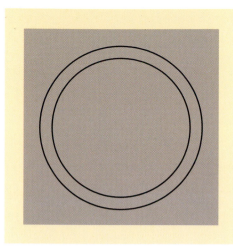

14 Drawing two circles

To make a shaded, concave round button, first use the centered-oval tool to draw 2 concentric circles, holding down the Shift key to constrain each to a perfect circle. Draw the smaller circle in front of the larger.

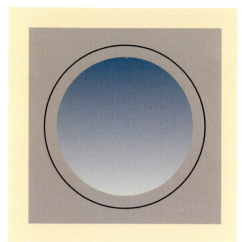

15 Creating an ellipse

Fill the inner circle with a vertical gradient from dark at the top to a lighter tone at the bottom.

16 Filling the outer circle with a gradation

Fill the outer circle with the same gradient, but with its angle rotated 180 degrees so that the light tone is at the top and the darker tone at the bottom.

17 Type a numeral

Use the type tool to type a numeral or letter and fill it with a medium tone.

18 Creating a shadow

Copy the numeral and paste it in front of the original. Fill it with a darker tone, and then move it down a few points.

19 Sending the shadow behind

Cut the darker numeral to the clipboard, select the original numeral, and choose Paste In Back to paste the dark numeral behind the original, creating a drop shadow.

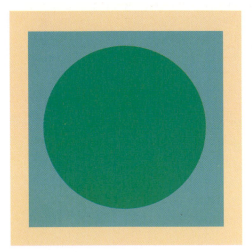

20 Drawing a circle
To create a rounded, convex button, first use the centered-oval tool with the Shift key held down to draw a perfect circle from the center outward. Fill the circle with a medium tone of color.

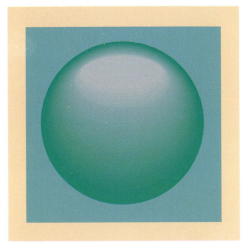

21 Creating an ellipse
Copy the circle and paste the copy in front of the original. Fill the copy with a lighter tone, and then scale it 50% horizontally and 20% vertically. Move this ellipse to the position shown.

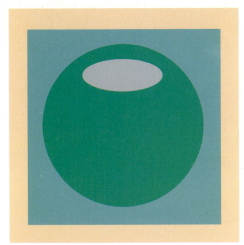

22 Blending between circle and ellipse
Use the blend tool to create a 20-step blend between the circle and the ellipse.

23 Rotating 45 degrees
While the blend is still selected, rotate it 45 degrees counterclockwise.

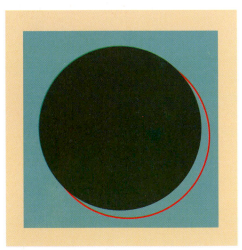

24 Creating circles for a drop shadow
Select the original circle, copy it, paste the copy in front, and fill the copy with a dark color. Copy the original circle again, move the copy a few points down and to the right, and then fill it with the same color as the background (a red outline has been added here to indicate the position of the second circle).

25 Blending between circles
Use the blend tool to execute a 20-step blend between these two circles.

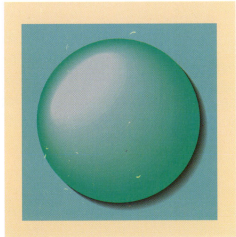

26 Sending the shadow behind
Cut the blend to the clipboard, select the original circle, and use the Paste In Back command to paste the blend behind the button.

27 Adding a numeral
Use the type tool to create a white numeral in the center of the button.

3

Creating a Custom Clip Art Illustration

Janet Ashford

Commercial clip art can be used without change to enliven a publication or an ad. But it can also be opened in Illustrator and edited to produce custom art by combining elements, changing colors, and adding type and backgrounds.

1 Choosing a clip art illustration

We began our poster illustration by opening the file called School.EPS from the Places & Faces 1 collection of PostScript clip art, part of the Images with Impact series produced by 3G Graphics. (The file, like most PostScript clip art, had been saved in an earlier Adobe Illustrator format so that it could be opened in the current version of either Illustrator or Aldus FreeHand.) The school image featured a borderlike arrangement of school buildings and trees colored in shades of gray.

2 Separating elements

The best clip art illustrations, like those produced by 3G Graphics, are composed of separate elements that can be isolated from the illustration and used on their own. By clicking on the school illustration we saw that it was grouped, so that the entire illustration became selected. We chose the Ungroup command to break it up into smaller subgroups (schoolhouse, outbuildings, trees, flagpole and so on) which could be separated from one another as shown above. Each of these elements could be ungrouped again into its separate components.

3 Isolating the schoolhouse
After ungrouping the illustration, we selected and deleted all the elements except the 2-storey schoolhouse and flagpole and then saved the illustration under a new name so as not to destroy the original file.

4 Stretching the schoolhouse
To make the schoolhouse taller, we ungrouped it, used the direct selection tool to select only the points at the top of the building, and dragged them upward. We then selected and copied a row of 6 windows and positioned 2 copies of the row over the new top half of the building.

5 Modifying the windows
We knew we would want to place other clip art elements into the windows. So to make them larger, we moved the smaller 2-paned windows toward each other in pairs.

6 Adding color
We added color to the schoolhouse by selecting each of its component parts and assigning a process color through the Paint Style dialog box. We also drew a purple rectangle over 1 of the windows, copied it, and positioned copies over all of the windows.

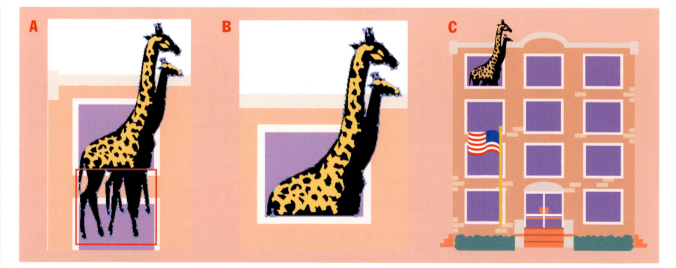

7 Opening a new illustration
Our plan was to fill each window space with a different graphic drawn from the Places and Faces 1 collection. We opened an Africa file, ungrouped the illustration, selected only the giraffes, and copied them to the clipboard.

8 Editing the giraffes
We scaled the giraffe illustration to the width of the window and positioned it over the window at the top left of the schoolhouse, so that the heads rose up above the building and the legs extended down below the window (A). We then drew a rectangle (shown in red) over the bottom half of the giraffes, with its top edge even with the bottom of the purple windowpane, selected

both the rectangle and the black background shape of the giraffe, and chose the Minus Front filter to truncate the giraffe shape (B). Now the giraffes looked like they were standing inside the building with their heads sticking out the window (C). Unwanted segments of a shape can be hidden by masking it, but using a Pathfinder filter to truncate it is easy and produces a file with fewer points and instructions.

9 Opening additional illustrations

To get elements to fill the rest of the windows, we opened 7 more illustrations from Places & Faces 1 including Egypt.EPS, Italy.EPS, USWashDC.EPS, Savanna.EPS, Jogging.EPS, UnderSea.EPS, and USNewYrk.EPS. The illustrations are shown here in their unedited form.

10 Creating separate elements

We ungrouped each of the illustrations shown in step 9, copied the parts we wanted to use, and pasted them into the schoolhouse illustration. We changed or added color to some of the separate elements to create the 11 illustrations we needed for the windows. Each element was scaled to fit the width of the windows.

11 Finishing the poster

We positioned the small illustrations in the windows and then darkened the building color slightly and moved the flagpole and flag to the right so they covered less of the windows. We completed the poster by drawing a pale purple background and black border around the illustration and added type in 54/44-point Times with a Horizontal Scale of 80%.

4

Drawing Three-Dimensional Boxes

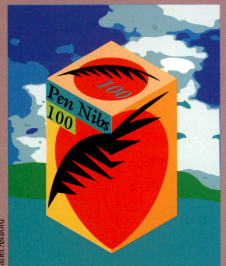

Janet Ashford

By applying the scale, shear, and rotate functions to the front, side, and top of an object, you can create 3-dimensional projections useful for illustration or for presentation of package designs. This example produces an isometric projection. Use the angles listed in the chart.

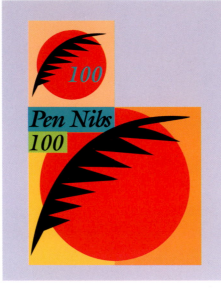

1 Drawing the flat elements
Start by using Illustrator to create art for the front, side, and top panels of your box.

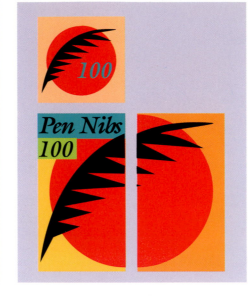

2 Separating the panels
If elements cross from 1 panel to another, cut these elements with the scissors tool so that each panel can be grouped as a separate unit.

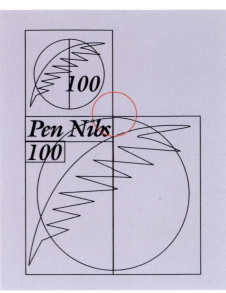

3 Positioning the panels
Position the panels so that their corners meet at a single point (see red circle), which will be a reference for all the following scale, shear, and rotate operations.

4 Scaling the top
Be sure to follow the steps in order. Select the top and scale it vertically to 86.602 percent.

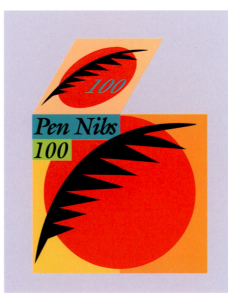

5 Shearing the top
Shear the top horizontally from the reference point by 30 degrees.

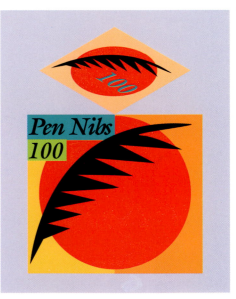

6 Rotating the top
Rotate the top by −30 degrees, using the reference point as the center of rotation. ⌘ *Negative values indicate clockwise rotation.*

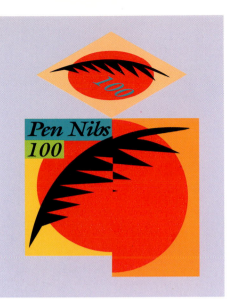

7 Scaling the front
Scale the front vertically by 86.602 percent.

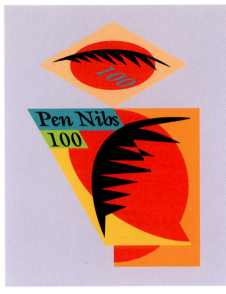

8 Shearing the front
Shear the front horizontally by −30 degrees from the reference point.

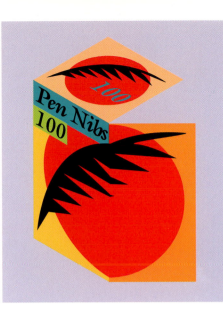

9 Rotating the front
Rotate the front −30 degrees, using the reference point as the center of rotation.

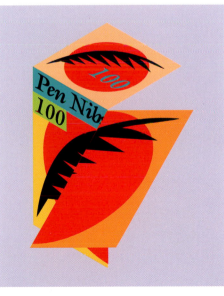

10 Scaling the side
Scale the side vertically by 86.602 percent.

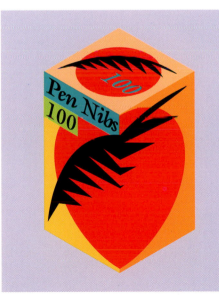

11 Shearing the side
Shear the side horizontally by 30 degrees from the reference point.

12 Rotating the side
Rotate the side 30 degrees, using the reference point as the center of rotation.

Chart of operations to produce isometric and trimetric projections

	Isometric		Trimetric	
TOP			**TOP**	
Vert. scale	86.602%		Vert. scale	70.711%
Horiz. shear	30°		Horiz. shear	45°
Rotate	−30°		Rotate	−15°
FRONT			**FRONT**	
Vert. scale	86.602%		Vert. scale	96.592%
Horiz. shear	−30°		Horiz. shear	−15°
Rotate	−30°		Rotate	−15°
SIDE			**SIDE**	
Vert. scale	86.602%		Vert. scale	86.602%
Horiz. shear	30°		Horiz. shear	30°
Rotate	30°		Rotate	30°

5

Converting a Photo to Line Art

Janet Ashford

An ordinary photograph can be transformed into a dramatic piece of PostScript art by autotracing a high-contrast version. You can use Illustrator to add color, line, and gradations.

1 Choosing a photo

To create a poster for a folk music camp, we started with a color photo of a drummer, taken by Peter Damashek. We planned to concentrate on the expressive central figure and eliminate the other background elements.

2 Cropping and converting to grayscale

The photo was scanned in grayscale mode at 150 dpi, using the scanner's selection outline to crop the image.

3 Autotracing an unedited scan

The scan was autotraced in Adobe Streamline, using a 50% threshold, which converted all the gray tones to either black or white PostScript shapes. But much detail was lost in the process.

4 Editing the scan

To better prepare the scan for autotracing, we opened the scan in Adobe Photoshop and first painted out the figures in the background. To increase detail for the next step, the resolution was increased to 600 dpi.

5 Increasing contrast in the details

To make sure the face would convert well to black-and-white art, we selected it with Photoshop's lasso tool and increased the contrast in this area.

6 Converting to high contrast

Still working in Photoshop, we increased the contrast of the whole image until all the gray levels were converted to either black or white. The brightness was decreased slightly to retain detail in the face and clothing.

A   B   C

7 Autotracing the edited scan

The edited scan was autotraced in Streamline, producing better detail in the figure. (It could also have been autotraced using the built-in autotrace function in Illustrator.) But when placed over a colored background, we saw that parts of the image were transparent or clear rather than white (A). We drew a white-filled rectangle (shown here with a red outline) (B) and pasted it in back of the illustration so that the white showed through the transparent areas (C). ⚫ *Illustrator's autotracing function, and Streamline when used in outline mode, convert a black-and-white bitmap to PostScript art by tracing around the black and white shapes, starting with the largest shapes and working in layers upward to the smallest shapes. In our image the large black shapes were traced first, followed by smaller white shapes on top.*

8 Varying the black-and-white art

To add a second color to the art, we selected the white background rectangle and changed its fill and stroke to deep yellow.

9 Finishing the second color

We then selected all the smaller white shapes and changed their fill and stroke to the same deep yellow color.

10 Using 2 colors

To create a 2-color version, we selected all the black shapes in the image and changed their fill and stroke to a blue composed of 75% of both cyan and magenta.

11 Using tints of a single color

Black-and-white art can also be colored using tints of a single color. We used a 75% tint of blue for the black areas and a 25% tint for the light areas.

12 Experimenting with color combinations

To make it easier to try different color combinations, we used the Select, Same Fill Color filter to select all of the light-colored shapes and then all of the dark shapes and change their fill and stroke colors as a group. We used

this method to create a version with related shades of brown and orange (A) and hotly contrasting shades of red and green (B).

13 Adding a contrasting stroke

Another way to vary the image is to specify the stroke in a contrasting color. Here we added a thin red stroke to the blue shapes.

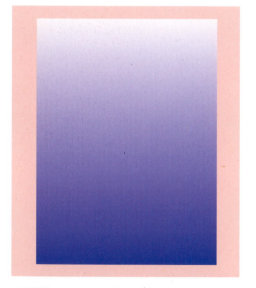

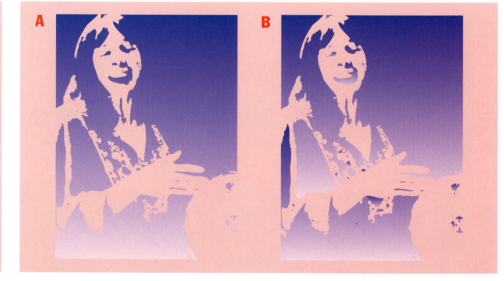

14 Filling shapes with gradations

To create a variation based on color gradations we selected the background rectangle and filled it with a linear gradient from sand color at the top to navy blue at the bottom.

15 Creating a compound path

To make all the black shapes into a compound path so that they could be filled with a gradient as a group, we selected the shapes and chose Compound Paths, Make from the Object menu.

16 Filling the black shapes with a gradient

We then selected the compound path, specified a stroke of None, and filled the path with a linear gradient from navy blue down to pink. The gradient spread through the shapes from the top to the bottom of the image (A).

If the black shapes had been filled with the blue to pink gradient without being first converted to a compound path, each separate shape would have been filled with the whole color range of the gradient, producing a different effect (B).

17 Combining the 2 gradients
The gradient in the black elements, when seen over the gradient in the background rectangle, produced an interesting solarized effect.

18 Selecting the small white shapes
We next selected all the smaller white shapes and made them into a compound path.

19 Filling the white shapes with a gradation
We filled the compounded white shapes with the same sand-to-navy blue gradation used for the background rectangle. The use of gradients gave a rich, mysterious look to otherwise simple line art.

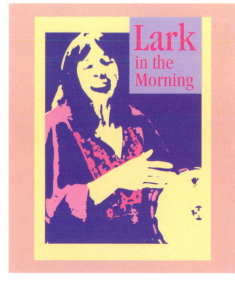

20 Creating a poster
To create a 3-color poster, we enlarged the background rectangle, filled it with pale yellow, filled the black areas with blue, and filled the smaller white shapes with tints of magenta

21 Drawing background shapes
To add more color interest to the clothing, we drew shapes over the areas where the clothing is transparent and filled them with tints of magenta.

22 Layering the colored shapes
We cut and pasted the magenta shapes in back of the blue shapes, so that they would show through the transparent areas.

23 Adding type
We completed the poster by drawing a rectangle filled with a tint of blue and positioned magenta type in Garamond Condensed over the rectangle.

6
Modifying Clip Art

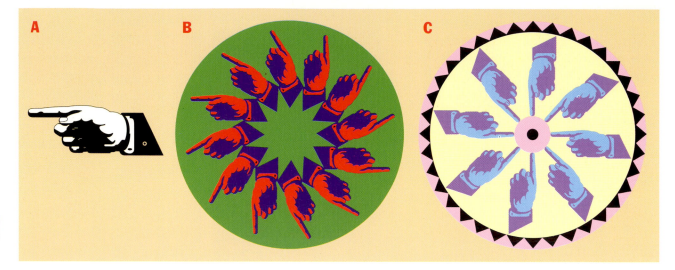

Janet Ashford

The transformations that can be applied to any graphic or text object can also be applied to PostScript clip art to produce a variety of effects. We used rotation, reflecting, coloring, and gradients to modify clip art. We also changed the stroke weight and color to produce custom variations and a neon effect.

Rotating

A single clip art element can be rotated to produce a circular design. We started with a hand from T/Maker's ClickArt EPS Illustrations (A) and colored it red and purple. We typed Command-C and -F (Copy and Paste In Front) to place a copy directly on top of the original and then chose the rotate tool, held down the Option key, clicked to the right and down from the sleeve of the hand to define the center of rotation, and entered a value of 30 degrees. We then typed Command-C, -F, and -D (Repeat Transform) to repeat the Copy, Paste In Front, and Rotate functions until we had 10 hands pointing outward from the same center (B). To create a variation we changed the colors, changed the center of rotation, and entered a value of 45 degrees to create 8 hands pointing inward (C). Backgrounds were added to both graphics.

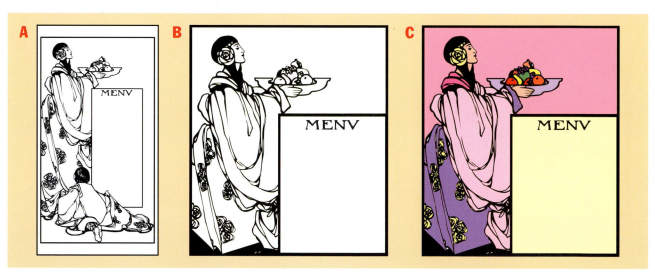

Flipping and coloring

To modify a menu design we started with an image from Silicon Designs' Art Nouveau Images (A). We deleted the outside rectangle frame and then cropped away the bottom third of the image by drawing a rectangle over the top 2 thirds, selecting all the elements, and applying the Crop filter. We then added a single thick black border by drawing a solid-filled black rectangle and pasting it in back of the illustration (B). We added color to the image by selecting the white shapes and changing their fill to various colors (C).

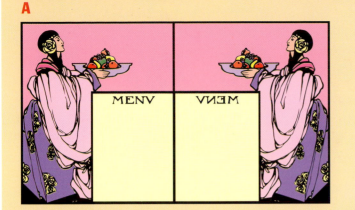

A

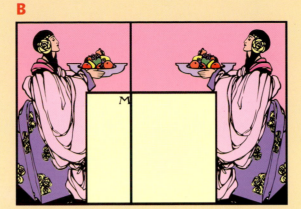

B

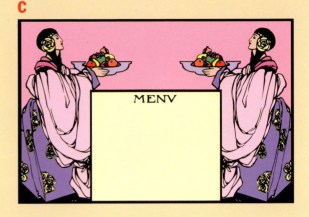

C

Expanding horizontally

We then selected the entire illustration and reflected it across the vertical axis, using its right edge as a reference point (A). We moved the reflected copy to the left and deleted the mirror-image lettering (B). Then to eliminate the unwanted vertical black line near the center, we deleted the black background rectangles around each of the illustration halves and drew a new, single black background rectangle behind them both. To complete the illustration, we selected the lettering, cut it, and pasted it in front (C).

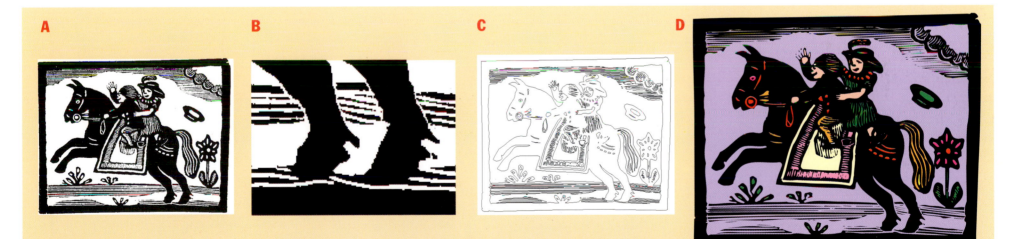

A   B   C   D

Autotracing scanned clip art

In addition to electronic clip art, printed clip art can be scanned and converted to EPS format for modification in Illustrator. We chose an illustration from *Pictorial Archive of Quaint Woodcuts in the Chap Book Style*, published by Dover Publications, scanned it at 200 dpi, and saved it as a bitmapped TIFF (A). We opened the image in Adobe Photoshop and drew with white along the edges of some of the forms (as with the legs of the horse) to separate them from background elements so that these would not be traced into a single object during the autotracing process (B). In order to quickly get a complete autotracing of the complex image, we opened the TIFF in Adobe Streamline, autotraced it in outline mode, and then opened the autotracing in Illustrator. Viewing it in Artwork mode shows the many outlines of which the image is composed (C). We added color to the picture by selecting the white shapes and changing their fills to colors (D). To create a variation, we filled some of the shapes with gradients, creating compound objects out of groups of shapes so that the gradient would appear to flow through them as a group (see opening art).

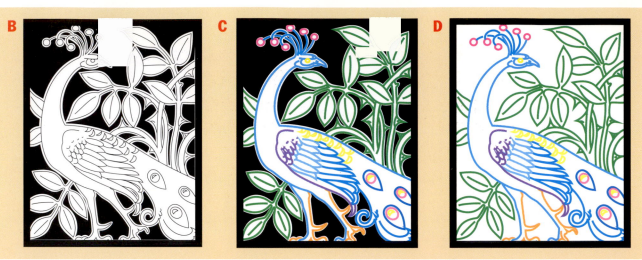

Changing the stroke

To create an illustration of a peacock, we began by opening another file from Silicon Designs' Art Nouveau Images (A). To crop the art we used the Crop filter to isolate the peacock and then drew a black rectangle with an 8-point stroke around the remaining image (B). We then selected all the thin lines that define the details of the illustration, increased their stroke weight to 2 points, and changed the colors of the strokes to fit the various objects — green for the leaves, blues for the peacock, and so on (C). To create a variation we selected all of the black shapes that define the background and deleted them (D).

Adding background shapes

To create another variation of the peacock illustration, we returned to a saved version of step C in "Changing the stroke" (above), selected all the black background shapes, and changed their fill to light blue. We changed the color of the border to a slightly darker shade of blue (A). We then selected all of the leaf shapes that were defined by open paths with endpoints that were near each other and filled them with yellow. ⌘ *When you specify a fill for a path that is not closed, Illustrator automatically draws a line between the 2 endpoints to create a closed shape.* We used the freehand tool to draw closed shapes over the remaining leaves, filled them with yellow, drew shapes over the peacock, and filled these with pink (B). We then cut and pasted all these shapes in back so that the detail strokes were once again at the top layer of the illustration (C). To create another variation we selected all the detail lines and shapes in the illustration and reduced their stroke weight to 1 point, which created gaps between the lines and the background shapes. We then gave the border rectangle a black stroke and fill, which showed through the gaps (D).

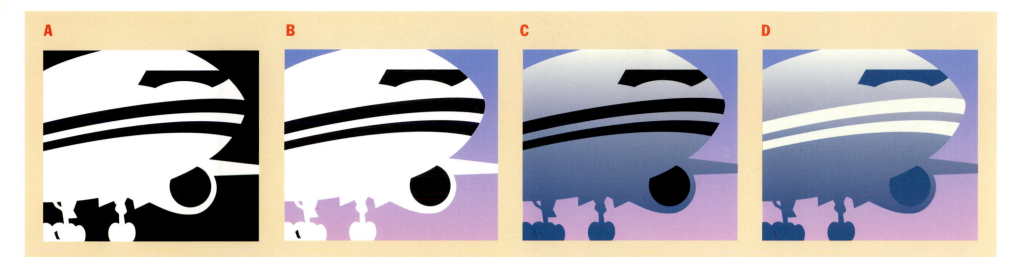

Adding gradients

Gradients can be used to add dramatic color effects to simple black-and-white graphics. We started with an airplane image from Dynamic Graphics' Designer's Club Ideas & Images clip art service (A). We selected the black background rectangle and filled it with a vertical linear gradient from blue down to pink, using the Gradient dialog box to define the starting and end-ing colors (B). We selected the white airplane shape and filled it with a vertical linear gradient from pale yellow down to dark blue (C). We then selected the 2 stripes on the airplane and filled them with the same pale yellow used to begin the airplane's gradient fill. We selected the remaining black shapes of the window, engine, and tire and filled them with the same dark blue used to end the airplane's gradient fill (D).

Creating a neon effect

To create a drawing suitable for a neon effect we first opened a cloud graphic from Dynamic Graphics' Designer's Club Ideas & Images (A). We added color to the graphic (B), and then simplified it by removing all but a single cloud shape and a single lightning shape (C). To apply a neon effect to the cloud shape, we copied it and pasted the copy in back, increased its stroke width and stroked and filled it with a slightly lighter shade of blue. We re-peated this process of creating copies, each with a wider stroke and lighter color until we had 5 cloud shapes stacked on top of each other, with the lightest shape at the back, giving the impression of a neon glow. We used the same procedure to add a neon effect to the lightning shapes (D).

7

Aiming for Efficiency

In creating JapanClips clip art, the artists of Matsuri Graphics make efficient use of many of Illustrator's automated drawing features — for example, dashed lines, pattern fills, and blending. And their use of Illustrator's grouping function also ensures that the buyers of the clip art get artwork they can use efficiently.

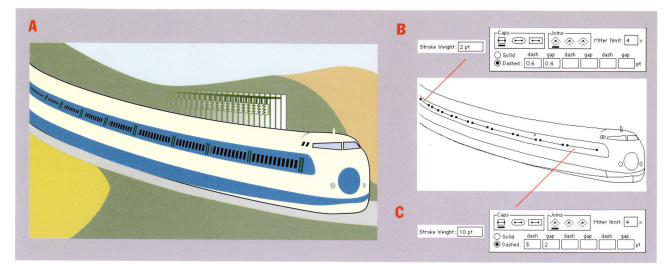

1 Using dashed lines

The windows of this train illustration (A) began as a single curved line with no end caps, which was then cut into shorter segments at the points where small vertical elements were drawn to indicate the breaks between cars. To make the windows, each line segment was then assigned a dashed pattern through the Paint Style dialog box. At the far end of the train a line weight of 2 points was used, with a dash length of 0.6 point and a gap of 0.4 point (B). The line thickness and the length of dashes and gaps increased for windows farther forward in the train. The second window's line weight was 3 points, the dash was 0.9 point, and the gap was 0.6 point. The progression continued, with line weights of 4, 5, 6, 7, 8, and 9 points, until the frontmost segment was given a weight of 10 points, a 3-point dash and a 2-point gap (C).

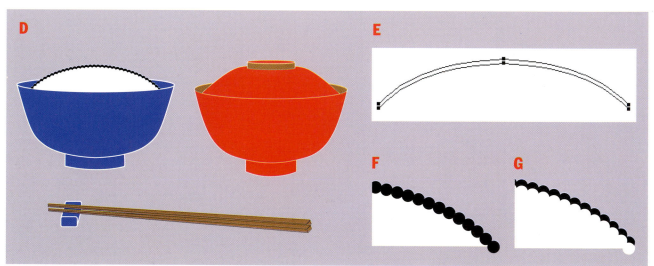

In an illustration of rice bowls (D), the rounded portion of rice was defined by 2 open curves. The first curve was drawn and then duplicated and moved down slightly (E). In the Paint Style dialog box the top curve was assigned round end caps, a black stroke, and a weight of 5 points (F). A dash length of 0 produced a line made up of perfectly round dots, and a gap of 4.5 points resulted in a very slight overlap between dots. Assigning the curve a white fill, even without closing the shape, filled in the mound of rice. When the second curve was assigned the same fill, weight, and dash pattern with a stroke color of white, the round dots that formed the curve overlapped the black dots to define the rice grains at the top at the top of the mound (G). ● *To make a dotted line, choose round end caps, choose Dashed for the stroke style, and assign a dash size of 0.*

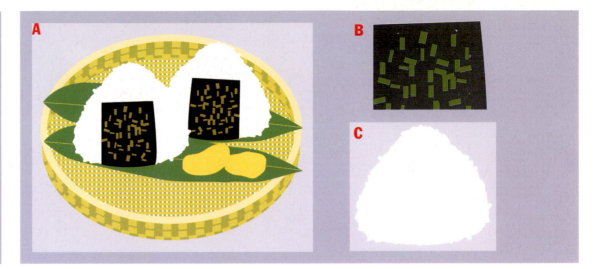

Layered lines were also used in the sekitei illustration (H). Each line was actually composed of 3 elements (I). A gray solid 6 -point line was overlaid by a 7-point white dashed line with round end caps, a dash length of 6 points, and a gap of 6 points so the dashes overlapped slightly. The dashed line "sculpted" a series of curved peaks on the top edge of the gray line (J). A duplicate white line was offset about 3 points to the left and overlaid to sculpt the bottom edge (K). Against a white background, the white lines disappear, leaving a series of scalloped gray lines.

2 Creating textures with lines

In an illustration of rice cakes on a round tray (A), the nori (seaweed) was defined as a black object textured with short flat-ended lines in a single green color but with different lengths and 3 different weights — 3, 4.5, and 6 points (B). The green flecks were all contained within the black shape that defined the trimmed sheet of nori. To make the gohan (rice), short white

lines with round end caps and a consistent weight (6 points) were used to define rice grains. A closed path filled with solid gray defined the shape of the mound and the shaded areas between the grains (C). Some of the rice grain lines extended beyond the edge of the gray shape to provide a bumpy surface texture.

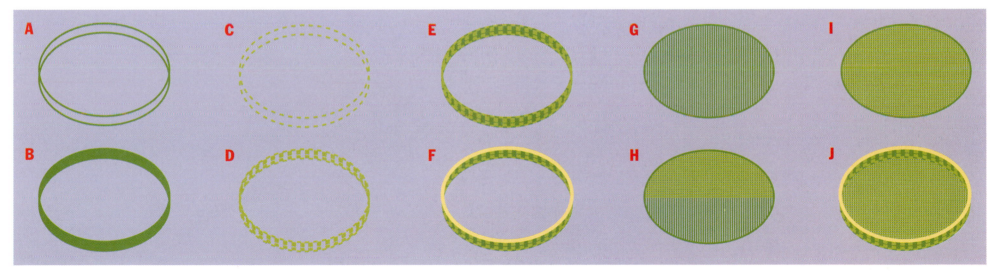

3 Blending lines

To create the bamboo tray shown in "Creating textures with lines" (above), an oval was drawn with the oval tool, assigned a green, 6-point stroke and no fill, and then duplicated by Option-dragging directly down, with the Shift key used to constrain motion (A). The identical green ovals created by a 7-step blend between the 2 original shapes overlapped to make a solid side wall for

the tray (B). Copies of the 2 original ovals were assigned a dashed pattern (weight, 6 points; dash, 15 points; gap, 15 points) in a lighter green (C), and were also blended in 7 steps; the blend was ungrouped, and a step near the middle was removed to leave a gap to add interest to the texture of the weave (D). Placing the patterned rings on top of the solid set completed the woven side wall of the tray (E). Changing the top ring to a 12-point solid stroke of

yellow provided a rim for the tray and also hid the construction detail at the points where the rings overlapped at the 2 sides of the tray (F). The bottom of the tray was assembled from a blend of vertical lines, trimmed to fit within the lowest oval (G) and then overlaid with a blend of horizontal lines, the top half built first (H) and then copied, pasted, and reflected (I), and finally grouped with the vertical grid and sent to the back to complete the tray (J).

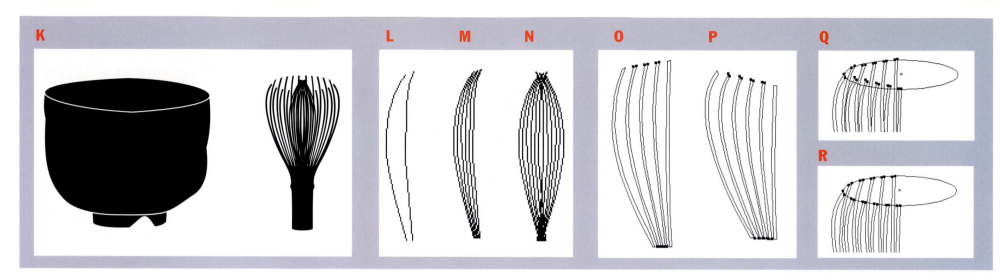

3 Blending lines, continued

Blended lines were used again to construct the core of the whisk in this illustration of the implements used for a tea ceremony (K). Two curves (L) serve as the basis for a 4-step blend (M). The blend was grouped with the original lines and the group was duplicated and flipped to complete the core (N). In contrast to the core, the outer ring of tines was constructed from 2 blends of thin closed shapes rather than from lines (O, P). Each of the original shapes used for the blend was made by duplicating an open curved path and then joining the original and the duplicate at their ends. An oval, which had been used to establish the positions of the top ends of the shapes originally used to make each of the blends, was fitted to the ring of tines (Q), and the top points were selected individually and moved down to make the tines conform to the oval (R).

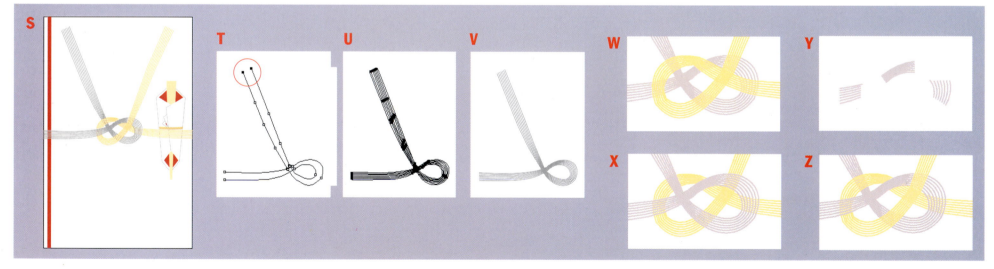

The cords in this illustration of a shuugi-bukuro envelope (S) are mirror images of each other. A cord was constructed by drawing the inner and outer curving threads, selecting the top end points of the 2 curves (T), and then clicking on these points with the blend tool to create the interior threads. Note that the 2 curves are constructed of different numbers of points. Therefore, although blending from the starting points resulted in the expected set of intermediate curves (U), choosing any other "pair" of points for blending would have generated a somewhat unpredictable and tangled-looking result. The set of silver curves (V) was grouped and duplicated, and the duplicate flipped across the vertical axis. The duplicate lines were selected and assigned a gold color, and moved into position on top of the silver set (W). To simulate the knot, another copy of the silver set was layered on top (X). Then the lines were cut and the excess portions deleted so that only the overlying parts of the knot remained, as shown here with only the remaining parts of the silver cord shown (Y); this created the appearance of interwoven cords (Z). Cutting away the unneeded parts didn't have to be an exacting task; the silver cord on the bottom layer exactly matched the 1 on top, and its threads merged perfectly to hide the cut ends.

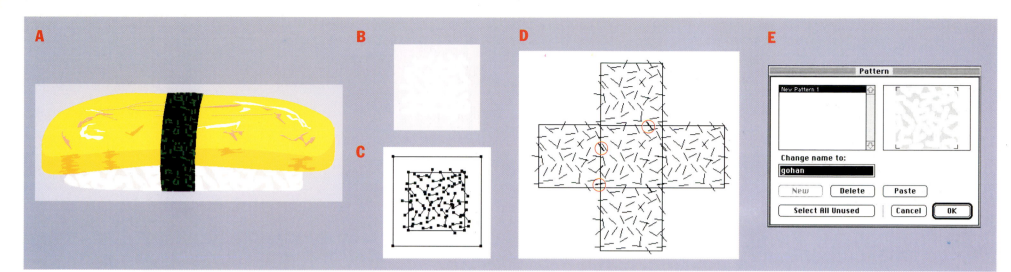

4 Creating patterns

Patterns make it easy to fill shapes with a particular design or texture. For the sushi shown in the opening illustration, patterns were used for the rice (gohan) and the seaweed (nori) (A). To make a nongeometric repeating pattern for the rice, a 0.083-inch long, white 4-point round-end line was drawn and copied, and the copies were pasted and rotated to various angles. A gray-filled rectangle provided a background (B). To define the repeating tile of the pattern, a no-stroke, no-fill rectangle that would "clip" the white lines and gray background was layered behind both (C). To make a pattern that repeats seamlessly, the elements at the top and bottom edges and at the right and left edges must be adjusted so they will connect and will thus camouflage the edges as the repeating tiles are laid next to each other. In designing a pattern, this overlap can be achieved by surrounding the pattern tile with copies of itself and arranging the elements at the edges to match. For the rice pattern, some of the rice grains at the edges (the elements shown inside the red circles) were aligned in this way (D). When the pattern was complete, the rice grains, background, and defining rectangle were selected, and then Object, Pattern, New was chosen so the pattern could be named and saved (E).

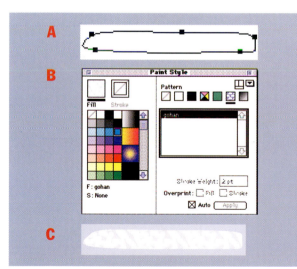

5 Filling an object with a pattern

Once a pattern is defined, the shape to be filled is selected (A), and the pattern name is chosen from the Pattern fill menu (B). The pattern automatically repeats to fill the selected shape (C). In the JapanClips series, the gohan pattern made it easier for the artist to create the artwork; it also provides buyers of the clip art with a pattern they can use in their own artwork.

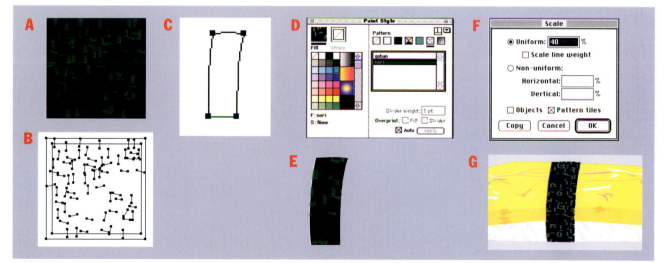

6 Modifying a pattern fill

The nori pattern was defined in much the same way as the gohan, except that the line segments were without end caps and they varied in length and thickness (A). Again, a no-stroke, no-fill rectangle was layered behind the other elements to define the pattern tile, clipping the green lines and black background that extended beyond its edges (B). Like the gohan, the nori pattern was defined in the Pattern dialog box. To apply the pattern, the seaweed strip was drawn (C), and the nori fill was assigned through the Paint Style dialog box (D). The pattern seemed too large at full size (E). To change the size of the pattern, you can select the pattern-filled object, Option-click it with the scale tool, enter a percent value, then select the Pattern Tiles box and deselect Objects (F) to change the size of the pattern fill only (G).

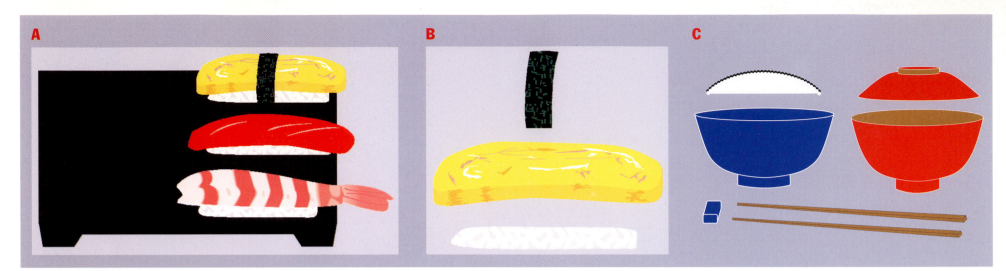

7 Grouping for efficiency

Like patterned fills, Illustrator's grouping function provides advantages for both the originator and the users of the artwork. In creating the JapanClips files, grouping was used to lock related objects together so they could be moved, copied, or modified efficiently. In many cases this grouping followed the same logic as the grouping used for the final files, where objects are grouped according to the way an artist is likely to use them. For instance, the entire Sushi file (shown on page 26) comprises a group. Choosing Arrange, Ungroup releases this overall grouping and results in 4 grouped objects: the table and 3 pieces of sushi, which can be controlled independently (A). Each piece of sushi can be further ungrouped into the elements from which it is assembled (B), and finally into individual lines and shapes.

The rice bowls illustration (shown on page 26) is grouped so that the 2 chopsticks, their rest, the 2 bowls, the mound of rice, and the cover of the dish can all be manipulated separately. Notice that the interiors of the bowls are drawn so that the bowls look complete with or without the rice or the lid in place (C).

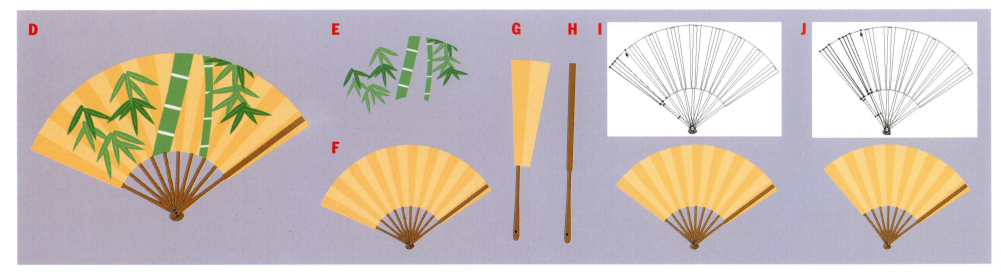

A fan illustration (D) within the JapanClips series is also grouped so it can be easily modified to be used in the way an artist might want to employ it. Ungrouping the fan allows the printed bamboo design (E) to be separated from the fan itself (F). Further ungrouping shows that the fan has been constructed from identical units composed of a brown rib with 2 paper rays attached (G), and a single rib by itself to serve as an end piece (H). This design makes it easy to fold the fan by selecting 1 of the fan segments and deleting it, or by clicking the rotation tool on the pivot point of the segment (the black spot where the ribs meet) and then dragging the segment clockwise to move this part of the fan on top of the next segment (I). Shift-selecting and deleting or rotating 2 segments at a time folds the fan farther (J). (Although this folding can be done by deleting the fan segments, rotating provides more flexibility for experimenting with the spread of the fan. Rotating segments instead of deleting them makes it possible to re-expand the fan easily, or to fold the fan in partial rather than full segments by rotating a segment only part of the way over the segment next to it.)

8

Outlining an Illustration

A heavy outline around the overall shape of an illustration, or part of it, can add punch to the artwork. Applying this style to related spot illustrations can also help to unify them.

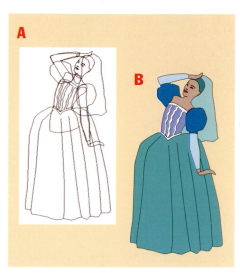

1 Preparing the artwork

Draw or import the artwork (A) and stroke and fill it according to the style you want to use (B). We used illustrations taken from 3G Graphics' People 1 collection of clip art.

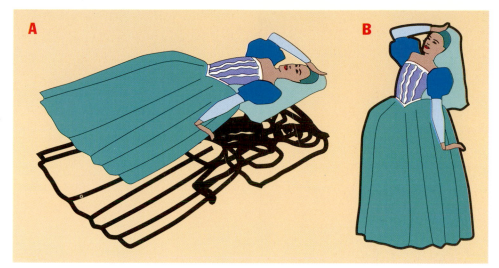

2 Thickening the outline

To thicken the outline at the perimeter without thickening the other strokes within the illustration, select and group all the parts of the illustration, copy this grouped object, and paste the copy behind the original. At this point the copy would be selected but would be hidden in back of the original. Use the Paint Style palette to assign a thicker stroke to the selected copy, shown here in an exploded view (A). Although the strokes throughout the illustration would thicken, they would be visible only at the perimeter, where they would extend beyond the original artwork (B).

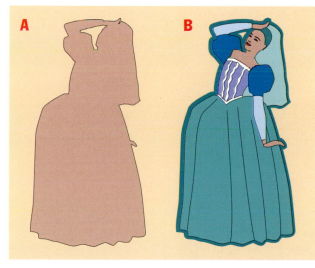

3 Using the Unite filter

Another way to create a thicker outline is to use the Unite filter from the Pathfinder filters. Select all the objects in the illustration and apply the filter. All the objects will be combined into a single path (A). Paste the new path behind the original artwork and assign a stroke width and color. We used a heavy blue stroke (B).

4 Modifying the outline

You can change the style, color, or width of the outline stroke by selecting it and using the Paint Style palette. We created a double outline by assigning a thick stroke to a perimeter outline created with the Unite filter and then assigning an even thicker stroke in a second color to a copy pasted in back (A). To create a scalloped effect, we specified a black dashed line with round end caps for the perimeter outline, then pasted a copy in back of it and specified a thicker, solid yellow stroke (B).

9

Blending Lines

David Smith

Designer/illustrator David Smith enjoyed using the computer to create artwork that couldn't be achieved any other way. This network of curves is based on a line-to-line blending technique that he developed.

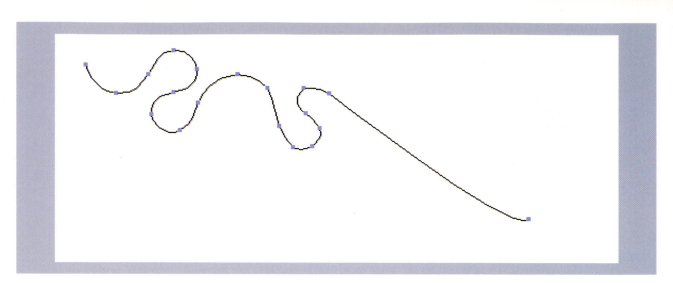

1 Drawing the first curve

The first step in creating a network of lines is to draw an interesting, smoothly flowing curve with large "loops" where the line balloons out. This curve will form 1 edge of the network. ⚫ *To keep a curve smooth, use the pen tool to draw with only a few control points, and keep the control levers for the curve points tangent to the line wherever possible.*

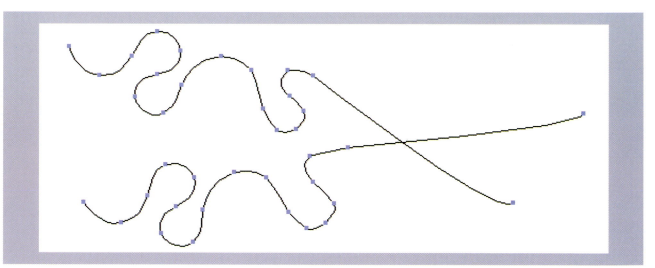

2 Shaping the second curve

Next the curve is selected and a copy is Option-dragged to form the other edge of the network. Making the second curve slightly different from the first will add interest to the network of lines. Offset or rotate the curve slightly, drag individual points into new positions, or reorient some of the control levers to reshape the curve. ⚫ *To drag a copy in a constrained vertical or horizontal direction or at a 45-degree angle, press the Shift key after you begin Option-dragging.*

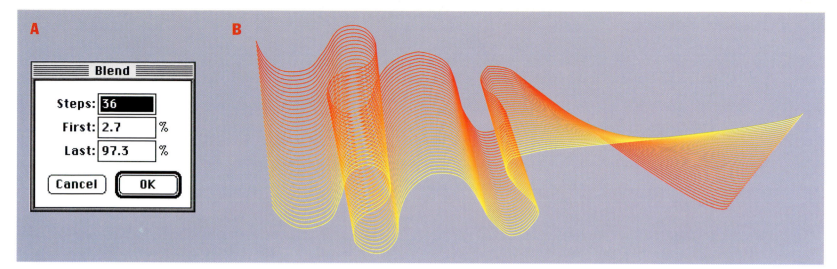

A

Blend

Steps: 36

First: 2.7 %

Last: 97.3 %

[Cancel]   [OK]

B

3 Blending the curves

In turn, select each curve and use the Paint Style dialog box to assign a color and weight for each of the 2 edges of the network; for this network, which is reduced here to about half its original size, we used 1-point lines in the default red and yellow of the Paint Style palette. Then generate the intermediate lines: Shift-click with the direct-selection tool on both curves to select all the points of both curves. With the blend tool, click once on corresponding single points of the 2 curves; we used the left endpoints of these 2 curves. The Blend dialog box will show the maximum number of color increments that Illustrator can produce between the 2 colors assigned to the starting lines, creating the most gradual color transition possible. Given the colors used here, the suggested number of steps was 254, which is the maximum allowable. Since the primary objective of this blend was to create an open network rather than to create a gradual color change, the number of steps was changed to 36 (A) to produce the desired degree of openness in the network (B).

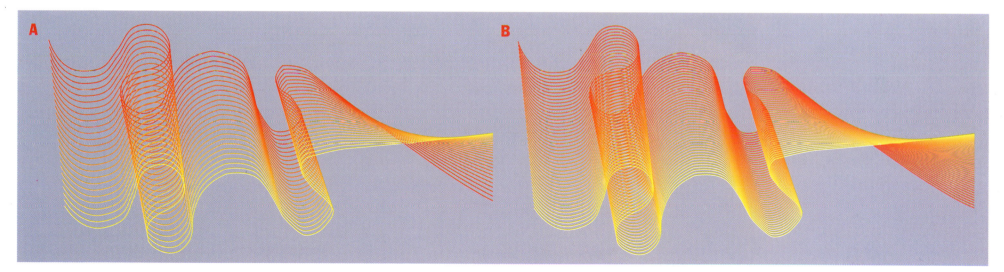

A

B

4 Trying different number of steps

The intermediate lines in a blend are created as a grouped object. By clicking anywhere on the group, you can select all the intermediate lines. These can then be removed by pressing the Delete key, and new numbers of steps can be tried. We tried 24 (A) and 45 steps (B) in order to vary the openness of the net and the appearance of the interference pattern generated as the curves cross each other.

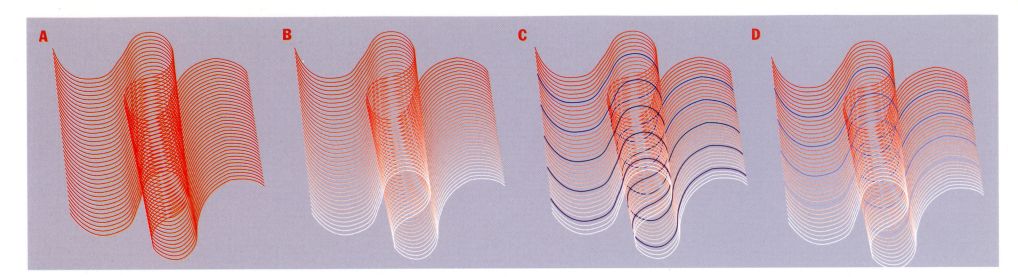

5 Experimenting with other color schemes

Once you understand how to create a blended network, there are numerous possibilities for assigning a color. For example, you can make a single-color network, blending between 2 lines of a single color (A). Or you can blend between tints of a single color (B). Or make the blend and then ungroup it and assign a contrasting color to some of the lines; for example, you can use either a single color (C), tints of a single color (D), or several different colors.

6 Using the network as a design element

David Smith used blue and purple curves (A) at the outer edges of a 42-line blended net in designing the artwork for the cassette J-card and the CD package for an album of music for the Hearts of Space recording label (B).

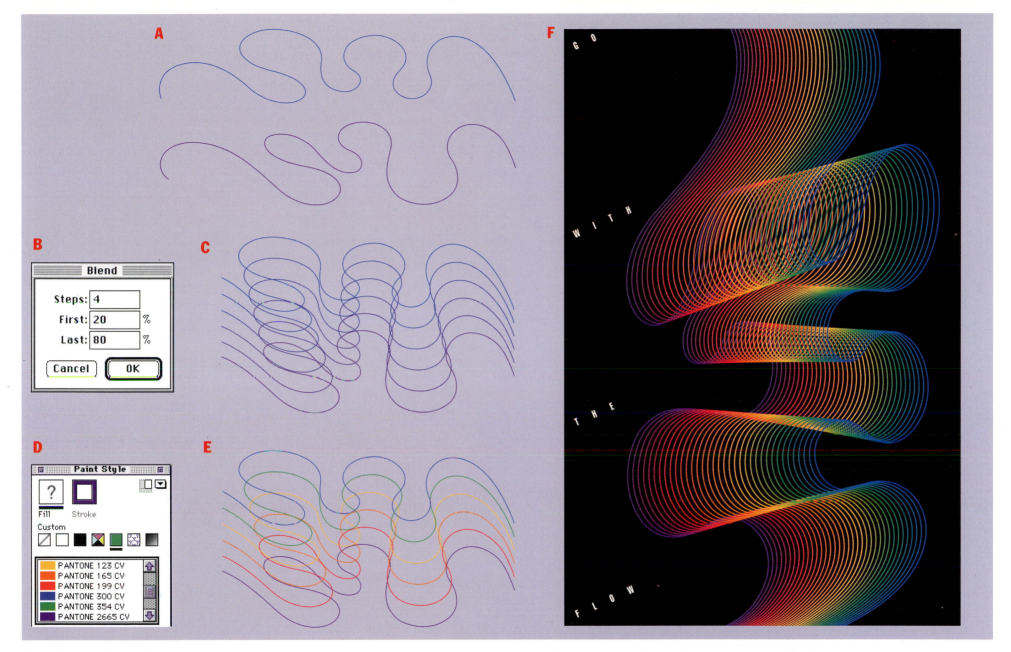

7 Creating a multicolor blend

If, instead of blending between 2 colors, you want to create a network whose lines undergo several color changes, you can start the process by drawing 2 initial curves (A) and then using a small number of steps (B) to make a blend (C). The number of steps should be the number of color changes you will want in the final multicolor blend; for this rainbow blend David Smith used a 4-step blend. Then ungroup this blend and use the Paint Style dialog box to assign a color to each of the intermediate lines. Smith used colors selected from the Pantone Custom Color palette (D) to set up a rainbow of color changes (E). Finally, blend from the first of these colored lines to the second, from the second to the third, and so on, using the same number of steps (in this case 6 steps) in each of the secondary blends; Smith used the finished blend (shown in the opening illustration) to create a poster that he titled "Go with the Flow," rotating the network to a vertical orientation, placing it on a black background, and adding scaled Helvetica Compressed type (F).

Janet Ashford

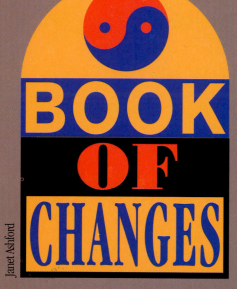

Illustrator's Paint Style palette makes it easy to create and use an infinite number of hues, tints, and shades that can be applied to graphic objects and type either as solids or as components of gradients and blends. Color wheels can be used to generate color combinations that work well to create different moods and styles.

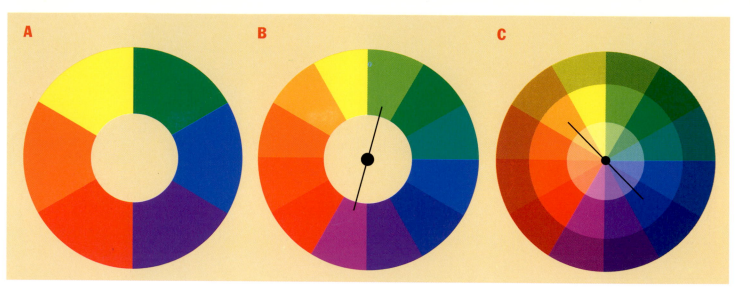

Working with a color wheel

In a color wheel hues are arranged around a circle in the order they appear in a rainbow. We created a basic wheel of 6 colors (A), using process colors specified in the Paint Style palette to reproduce traditional paint pigments. The primary colors (red, yellow, and blue) alternate with the secondary colors (orange, green, and violet). A color wheel with smaller subdivisions, like this 12-color version (B), can be used to locate pairs, triads, or larger groups of colors that produce pleasing combinations. A 3-part color wheel (C) can be used to find groups of colors, tints, and shades that work well together. The inner circle includes 50% tints, while the outer circle of shades was created by adding 15% black to the CMYK specifications for each hue.

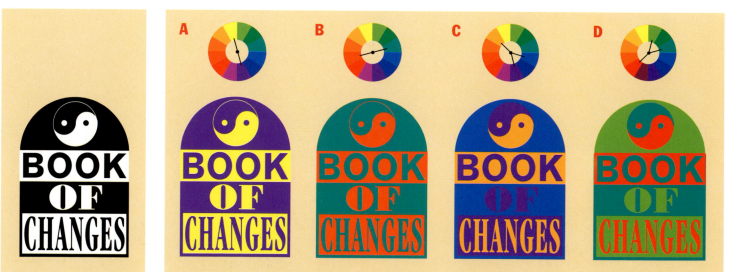

Varying a 2-color design

To demonstrate the use of color we started by creating a simple type design in black and white.

Using complements and near complements

Varying the color in a single illustration shows how different colors and combinations of color affect the mood of a piece. *Complementary colors* are pairs that are directly opposite each other on a color wheel (A, B). A pleasing group of 3 colors can be created by combining a color with the 2 colors on either side of its complement. These are called *near complements* (C, D). The colors in this and the following examples were chosen from the 12-color wheel shown in step 1.

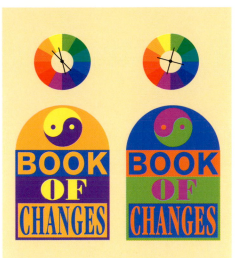

Combining double complements

Pairs of complementary colors can be combined to produce *double complements*, groups of 4 colors that look harmonious together.

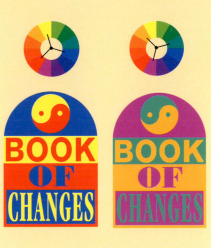

Combining triadic complements

Pleasing combinations can also be created by choosing *triadic complements*, 3 colors that are equidistant from each other around the color wheel.

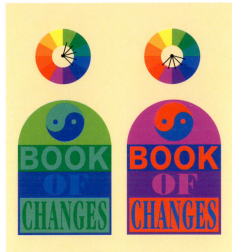

Combining multiple complements

Multiple complements are groups of 3, 4, 5, or more colors that are adjacent to each other on a 12-color wheel.

Using pastels

Another way to produce pleasing color combinations is by combining colors that have similar tint values. We created 2 combinations in pale, pastel tints using both double complements and multiple complements.

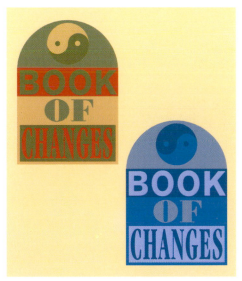

Using muted tones

Muted tones work well together, as in these combinations of warm red and yellow-green tones and cool tones of blue. To "mute" colors, increase the percentage of the smallest CMY component (cyan, magenta, or yellow).

Combining brights with neutral tones

Highly muted, or neutral, tones, including grays and muted tones of color, create an effective balance when combined with bright, highly saturated colors.

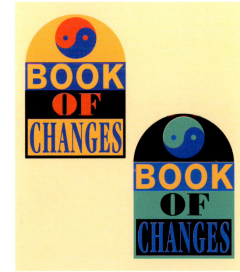

Setting off brights with black

Bright colors look even brighter when set off by black. Black can be used either for foreground subjects or as a background.

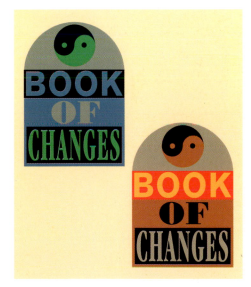

Combining brights, neutrals, and blacks

Another kind of combination that produces a rich color feeling is that of muted, neutral tones with black and accents of bright color.

11

Softening the PostScript Line

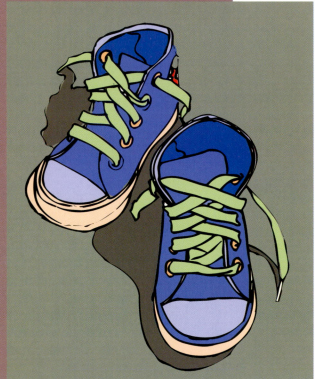

Janet Ashford

A variety of means, including tracing over templates, using the brush tool, and using filters, can produce an irregular line that is in certain circumstances softer and more appealing than lines of uniform weight.

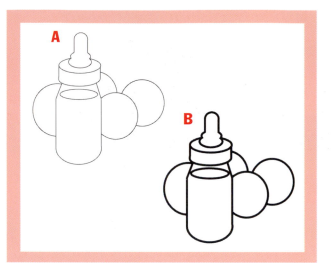

Using uniform line weights

PostScript illustration programs like Adobe Illustrator were originally designed to make technical illustration easier by producing lines of uniform width. Uniform lines make drawings look clear and crisp and can be easily changed in weight, from 1 point (A) to 4 points (B), for example, as in these drawings of a baby bottle with oranges.

Tracing a scanned drawing

But sometimes uniform lines look too formal, especially in editorial illustrations. In these cases, the irregular lines produced by natural media like pencil or pen are more appealing, as in this hand-drawn version of the baby bottle illustration. To bring the hand-drawn quality into Illustrator we scanned the drawing and saved it as a 72 dpi PICT for use as a template.

We opened the scan as a template in Illustrator and used the freehand tool to trace around the thick black lines to produce closed paths filled with black. The tracing is shown here in Artwork mode.

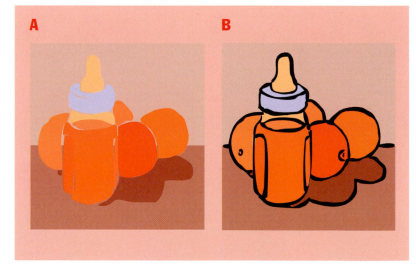

To add color to the drawing we again used the freehand tool to draw shapes on top of the black elements and filled them with appropriate colors (A). We then selected all the colored shapes, cut them to the clipboard, and chose Paste In Back to paste them in back of the black shapes that define the lines of the illustration. We added a background (B).

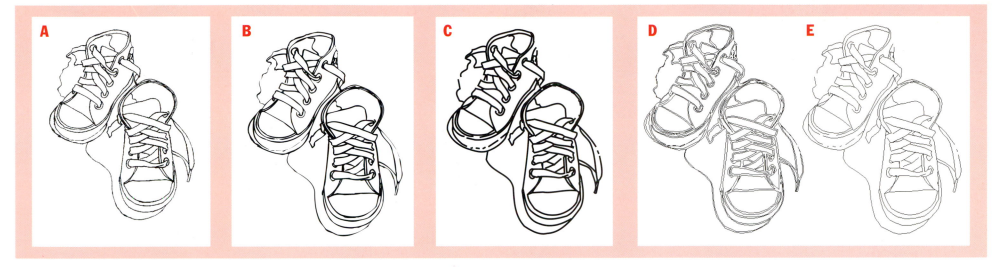

Autotracing a scanned drawing

Some drawings are too complex to be easily traced by hand in Illustrator. To get better, faster results with a complex pencil drawing we scanned it (A), and then used Streamline to make an outline autotracing, and for comparison, a centerline tracing. The outline autotracing (B) renders the black lines in the scan by drawing white shapes and layering them over black background shapes, as opposed to drawing objects in the shapes of the black lines themselves, as we did by hand in the previous example. The outlining process, though different from hand-tracing, captures the thick-and-thin variations of the line, whereas the centerline tracing (C) places a line of uniform width (a 2-point line in this example) along all of the lines of the scan. A view in Artwork mode shows the difference between the 2 types of autotracing. Only the outline mode tracing (D) retains the characteristics of the hand-drawn line by rendering them using shapes rather than as uniform lines (E). To add color, we selected the white shapes in the outline autotracing and changed their fills to various colors (see opening art).

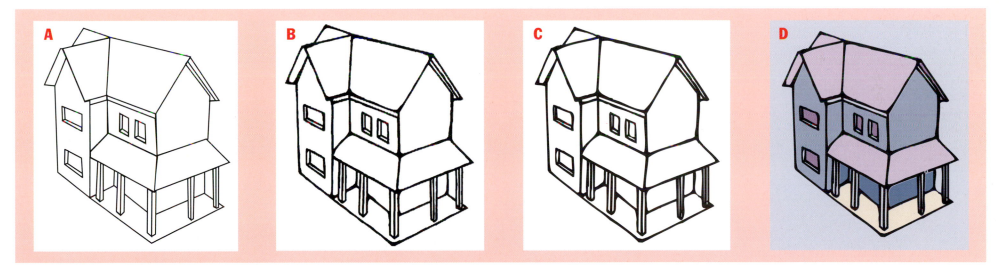

Alternating between PostScript and paint

Another way to soften the uniform PostScript line is to work back and forth between Illustrator and a paint program like Adobe Photoshop. We began by using Illustrator to draw a wooden toy house by tracing over a scanned photograph with the pen tool (A). We then opened the Illustrator EPS file in Photoshop and used its brush tool to thicken and embellish the line (B). We used Adobe Streamline to make an outline autotracing of the new bitmapped image (C). Streamline rendered the drawing by layering white shapes on top of black shapes. We opened the autotracing in Illustrator and added color by selecting the white shapes and changing their fills to various colors (D).

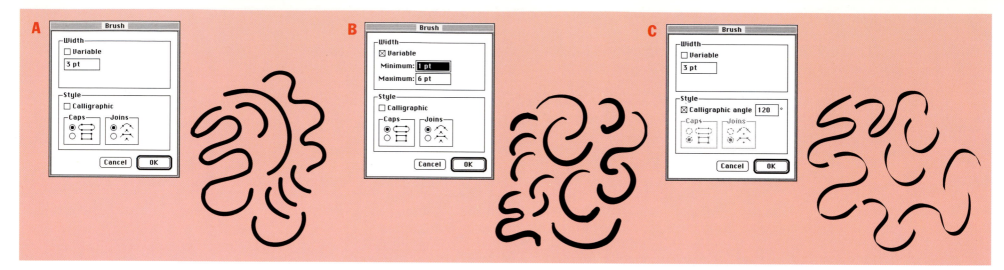

Using the brush tool

Responding to the need for variable lines, Illustrator now includes a brush tool that makes it possible to create 3 types of brush strokes by setting parameters in the Brush dialog box. Shown here are the dialog box settings and samples for a 3-point brush stroke (A), a 1- to 6-point variable brush stroke (B), and a 3-point, 120 degree calligraphic brush stroke (C). In each case, Illustrator shows the characteristics of the brush strokes or styles as you draw, then immediately converts them to closed shapes when the mouse is released. The variable brush must be used with a pressure-sensitive tablet and stylus. Responding to pressure on the tablet, the thickness of the stroke increases or decreases within the maximum and minimum line width values that have been entered in the Brush dialog box. The calligraphic brush imitates the look of strokes drawn with a straight-edged calligraphy pen. The angle of the pen nib can be varied in the dialog box, with the default set at 120 degrees.

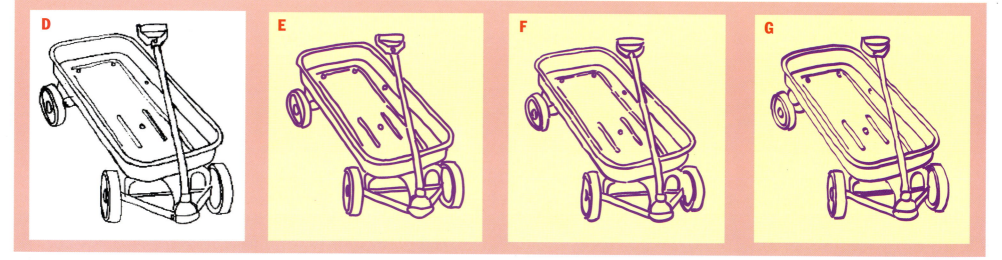

To render a drawing of a child's wagon, we scanned it for use as a template (D) and then drew over the scan by hand using the brush tool at the same 3 settings shown in the previous figures: as a 3-point stroke (E), a 1- to 6-point variable brush (F), and a 3-point, 120 degree calligraphic brush (G).

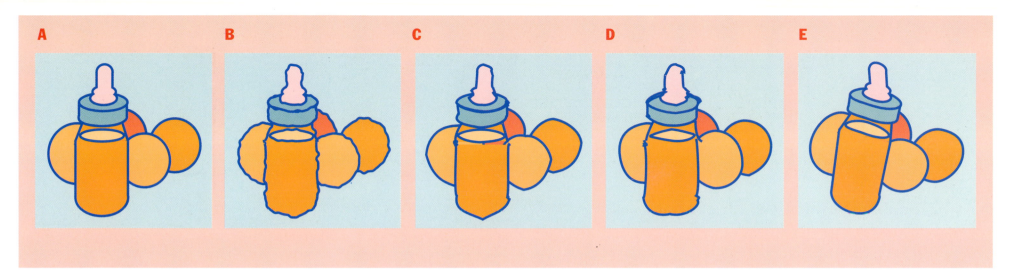

Applying Distort filters

The Distort filters, available under the Filter menu, can be used to vary the look of a uniform-line drawing by moving anchor points away from the original path in a number of different ways. The amount of distortion can be controlled by setting a percentage of distortion and other parameters in a dialog box for each filter. We applied 4 Distort filters to the same 3-point line drawing (A) to produce different effects. The Roughen filter moves anchor points away from the path in a jagged way. We applied the filter at 2%, clicking on Rounded rather than Jagged (B). The Scribble filter moves points away from the path in a random way. We used it with a setting of 5% for both horizontal and vertical movement (C). The Tweak filter moves anchor points away from the path by an amount that you specify. We used the filter at its default values of 5% horizontal and vertical (D). The Twirl filter alters a line drawing by rotating it more sharply at its center than at its edges. We used the filter with a setting of 25 degrees (E).

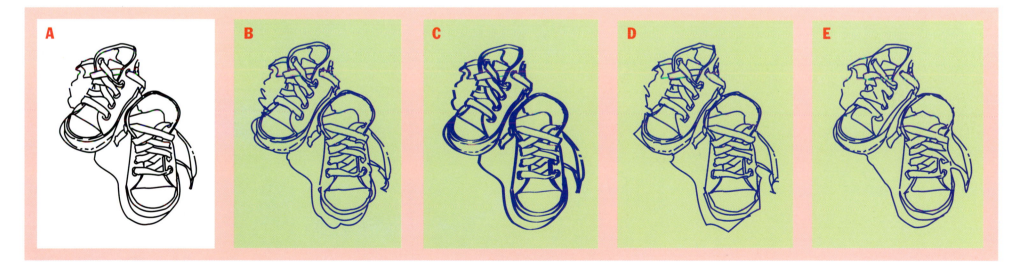

Using Stylize filters

We applied all the 6 Stylize filters to the same 2-point line drawing (A), and found that 4 of them produced pleasing results. The Bloat filter curves paths outward from their anchor points, using an angle determined by the value entered in the Bloat dialog box for Percent Bloat. We used the filter at 5% (B). The Calligraphy filter applies a calligraphic stroke to the existing paths in a drawing. We used it with an angle of 180 degrees with the drawing's strokes increased to 3 points (C). The Punk filter moves anchor points in a jagged way. We applied it with a value of 5 % (D). The Round Corners filter converts all the corner points of a path to points with smooth curves. We used the filter with a 10-point radius, used to determine the shape of the curves (E). The other 2 Stylize filters — Arrowhead, which adds an arrowhead to any selected line; and Drop Shadow, which creates a 3-dimensional shadow effect — were not appropriate for the attributes of the original drawing.

12

Creating a Posterization

Janet Ashford

By autotracing a grayscale scan to create a 4-level posterization, you can easily experiment with color changes and produce clean, stylized art at any size. Careful editing of the photo before posterizing ensures the best image.

1 Choosing a photo

To create a posterized image, we started with an original color photograph, taken by Peter Damashek, of American harp player Chris Caswell.

2 Cropping and converting to grayscale

The photo was scanned in grayscale mode at 150 dpi, using the scanner's selection outline to crop the image. Cropping helped to focus attention on the figure and eliminate distracting details.

3 Editing the photo to improve contrast

In order to get the best result from the autotracing process, we first opened the scan in Adobe Photoshop, darkened the area of the harpist's shirt, and increased the overall contrast of the image.

4 Autotracing with Streamline

Adobe Streamline, the program dedicated to autotracing and designed as an adjunct to Adobe Illustrator, can be used to autotrace either black-and-white line art or grayscale images. We chose Gray To Bitmap from Streamline's Edit menu and checked 4-level posterization with medium smoothing.

5 Opening the autotracing in Illustrator
Streamline analyzed the grayscale image and reduced its 256 gray levels down to only 4 levels. Opening the autotracing in Illustrator, we found that the image now consisted of shapes filled with either 12, 38, 63, or 87%

black (A). An exploded view shows how the image is constructed of many shapes layered over each other (B).

6 Using the Same Fill Color filter
To add color to the image, we began by selecting 1 of the dark gray shapes. We chose Select, Same Fill Color from the Filter menu, which automatically selected all the shapes with the same 87% black fill (A). We clicked on

the darkest of 4 shades of blue available through the preset paint swatches in the Paint Style dialog box (100 cyan and 100 magenta) to change both the fill and stroke of the shapes to dark blue (B).

7 Changing the gray levels to color
We continued adding color to the image by selecting a single shape of each of the remaining 3 gray levels and then using the Same Fill Color filter to select all the shapes with that fill. We changed the fill and stroke of all

the shapes in each group to a corresponding tint of blue chosen from the paint swatches. The figures show the conversion of 63K to 75C, 75M (A), of 38K to 50C, 50M (B), and of 12K to 25C, 25M (C). 🍎 *Shapes sharing the same fill and stroke can be grouped to make selec-*

tion easier, but grouping can disturb their stacking order if shapes with the same fill are layered both above and below shapes with a different colored fill. In this case the Same Fill Color filter is the best selection tool.

8 Creating color variations
The Same Fill Color filter makes it easy to experiment with color variations. Using this filter to quickly select shapes that shared the same fill, we created variations with warm tones (above) and cool tones (opening art).

Lin Wilson

One way to imply motion in an illustration is to add "action spikes" to the outlines of objects, as illustrator Lin Wilson did in this drawing of an Apple PowerBook "in flight."

20 K

100 K   **6 C, 15 Y, 34 K**

8 C, 23 Y, 56 K   **50 C, 100 K**

1 Drawing the object

It's possible to draw the action spikes as part of the original outlines for the artwork; but to keep the lines of the drawing smooth and straight, it's easier to draw the undistorted objects first and then add the spikes. To produce illustrations that print efficiently, Lin Wilson composes his artwork of simple shapes whenever possible, using minimum numbers of points (A). The PowerBook drawing is composed of layered no-stroke objects filled with 4 different grays and black (B).

2 Adding points for a spike

It takes 3 points to make each spike — 2 to anchor the base and 1 to make the tip. Clicking on a selected object's outline with the add-anchor-point tool creates the necessary points.

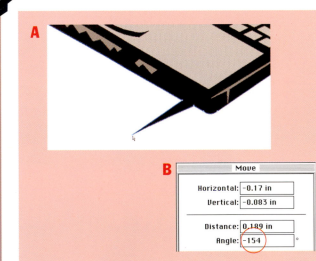

Move

Horizontal:	-0.17 in
Vertical:	-0.083 in
Distance:	0.189 in
Angle:	-154 °

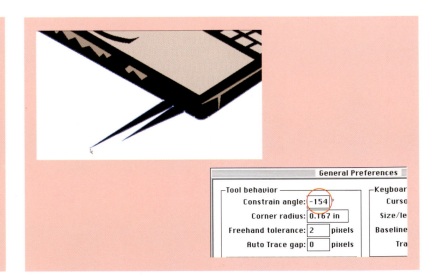

General Preferences

Tool behavior

Constrain angle:	-154 °
Corner radius:	0.167 in
Freehand tolerance:	2 pixels
Auto Trace gap:	0 pixels

3 Drawing out the spikes

To show movement in a particular direction, you can extend all the spikes at the same angle. Wilson's spikes trail to the left and down to show movement to the right and up. Drag the tip with the direct selection tool to draw out the first spike in the direction you want (A). Then you can determine its angle by opening the Move dialog box and reading the Angle value (B).

4 Constraining the angle of the spikes

In Illustrator, depressing the Shift key while you drag a point constrains movement to a vertical, horizontal, or diagonal direction. To change the angles that Illustrator uses for these directions, choose Preferences from the File menu and then choose General from the pop-out submenu. Change the Constrain Angle value to the value you found in step 3. Now when you depress the Shift key while dragging, the tip will be extended at the same angle as the first spike.

14

Showing Motion: 2

Jill Davis

A speed blur can be used to indicate motion, as shown here for a sphere speeding from left to right. In a technique developed by designer Jill Davis, the blur is accomplished by creating a blend between the speeding object and the background.

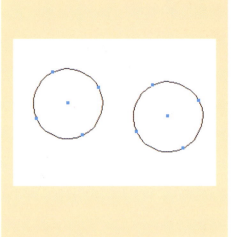

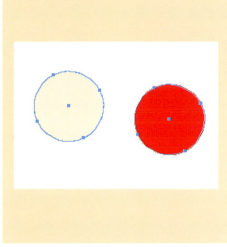

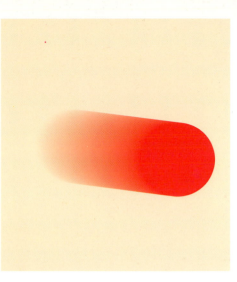

1 Establishing size and direction

Draw the shape of the speeding object, copy it, paste, and move the pasted copy into position where you want the speed blur to start. Select each shape in turn and use the Arrange menu to bring the speeding object to the front and to send the start of the blur to the back.

2 Adding color

Give the back object a solid fill of the background color. Give the front object a fill of another color. It isn't possible to blend between gradient-filled objects, so use a solid fill of the object's main color. A gradient (as in our example) can be added after blending if you like.

3 Blending

Select both objects, choose the blend tool from the toolbox, and use it to click a corresponding point on each of the 2 shapes. When the Blend dialog box opens, click OK to accept the number of steps Illustrator has suggested.

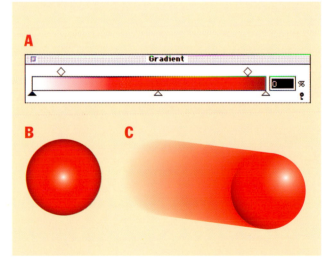

4 Adding detail

At this point you can change the fill of the speeding object if you like. Click on the object with the selection tool and then change the selected object's fill through the Paint Style menu. We defined a gradient fill through the Gradient dialog box (A), assigned it to the object (B), and then dragged the gradient tool across the object to offset the center of the gradient (C).

5 Experimenting with variations

To make the object appear to be speeding toward the viewer (A), we reduced the background-colored object to 75% of its original size before we blended. To make the speeding object's path appear to cross 2 backgrounds (B), we made the original tan-to-red blend and a green-to-red blend exactly on top of it; we copied the green background rectangle, pasted the copy on top of the blend, and then selected the blend and top rectangle and chose Masks, Make from the Object menu.

15

Using the Mosaic and Colors Filters

Janet Ashford

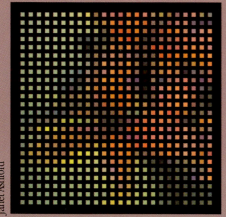

Illustrator's Mosaic filter can be used to create an interesting design and also to generate a palette of related colors. Colors can be modified using the Colors filters.

A

B

C

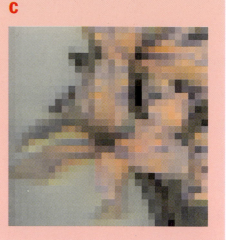

Using the Mosaic filter

The Mosaic filter converts a bitmapped PICT image into a PostScript image by clustering pixels of similar color into individual square tiles making up a grid. To use the filter on an image of flowers, we chose Create from the Filters menu and Mosaic from the submenu and chose the PICT to be converted (A). The Mosaic dialog box then appeared, showing the size of the PICT in points with default values for converting it to a new size, and for specifying the number of tiles desired, the spacing between the tiles, and other parameters (B). We used the default values to convert the image into a 30 x 30 grid of squares. The definition of the flower is barely suggested by the mosaic pattern, creating a soft image that might be used as a background (C).

A

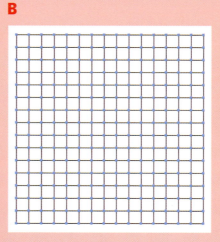

B

C

Varying the mosaic

We applied the Mosaic filter to the flower image again, specifying a 15 x 15 tile grid (A). A view in Artwork mode shows how the image is made up of small squares (B). We applied the filter again, specifying a 1-point space between the squares by entering a 1 in both the Width and the Height fields under Tile Spacing. This created a grid of squares with 1-point gaps between them (C). We used a similar method to create the opening art, starting with a more highly saturated version of the original flower image, creating a 24 x 24 grid with 1-point gaps, and placing it over a black background.

A **B** **C**

Using a mosaic to generate a color palette

Creating a custom color palette by specifying process colors individually can be tedious. But converting a color PICT to a mosaic makes it possible to use the range and subtlety of tones in a scanned photograph to quickly generate a group of new colors for use in the Paint Style palette. We opened the 30 x 30 mosaic grid made from the flower image (A), selected various squares, and assigned their colors to the paint swatches in the palette. We then used Adobe Streamline to convert the original PICT image of the flowers to a 4-level posterization (B), used the Same Fill Color filter to select all the objects with the same fill color, and filled them with new colors drawn from the new paint swatches we had created using the flower mosaic (C). ● *To "capture" a color from an object, select the object and then Option-click on a paint swatch. The color fill from the selected object appears in the paint swatch square.*

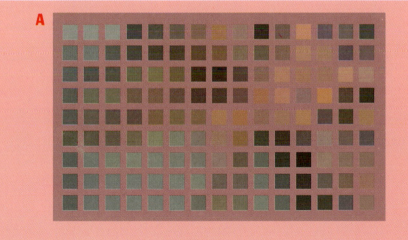

A

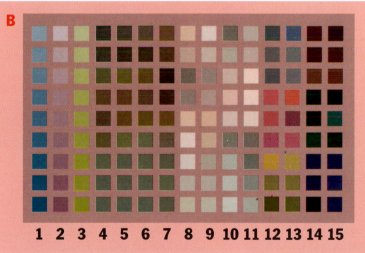

B

1 2 3 4 5 6 7 8 9 10 11 12 13 14 15

Using the Colors filters

The Colors filters make it possible to quickly change the color specifications of a selected object or group of objects. To create new colors that could be assigned to the Paint Style palette, we started with the bottom part of the flower mosaic created on the previous page (A) and edited the colors using a number of filters (B). We used the Adjust Colors filter to increase the cyan, magenta, and yellow components respectively of the bottom squares in columns 1, 2, and 3. We then selected all the squares in column 1 and used the Blend Vertically filter so that the squares between the top and bottom contained a series of intermediate colors. We repeated the blend process for columns 2 and 3. We next selected all the squares in columns 4–7 and applied the Saturate filter twice. This intensified the colors by increasing their CMYK components. We applied the Desaturate filter twice to columns 8–11, which decreased the CMYK components. In columns 12–15, we selected the top, middle and bottom groups of 12 squares and used the Adjust Colors filter to increase the cyan, magenta, and yellow components respectively in each group. We again selected the last 2 columns, 14 and 15, and used the Invert Colors filter to convert these colors to their color negatives.

16

Using the Pathfinder Filters

Janet Ashford

The filters provided under the Pathfinder filter submenu make it easy and fast to combine or divide overlapped objects, symbols, and type to produce new paths.

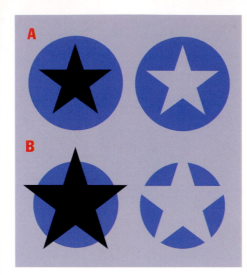

The Minus Front filter

This filter subtracts the object in front from the object in back, leaving a transparent "hole." We placed a small star over a circle and applied the filter to produce a star-shaped hole (A). When the object in front is larger than the object in back, its edges are clipped by the filter (B).

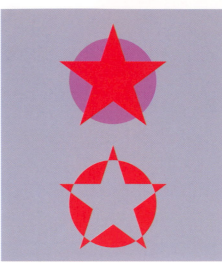

The Exclude filter

This filter knocks out the area where the front and back objects overlap, but unlike the Minus Front filter, it retains those areas in which the front object extends beyond the edges of the back object. The new path is automatically filled with the color of the original front object.

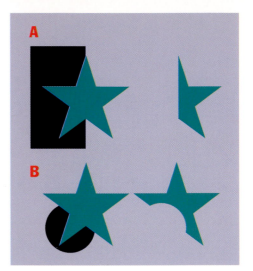

The Minus Back filter

This filter subtracts the object in back from the object in front. It can be used to quickly cut an object in half, as with this star (A) or to carve into an object using a curved edge (B).

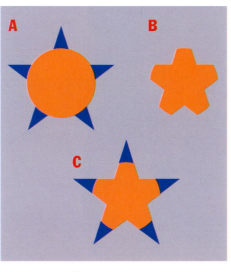

The Intersect filter

This filter creates a new object out of the intersection, or area of overlap between 2 objects, as between this circle and star (A). We placed a copy of the new object (B) over a copy of the original star to create the look of a 2-toned star (C).

The Unite filter

This filter combines 2 overlapped objects (A) to create a single shape (B).

Setting the Pathfinder Options filter

You can choose Pathfinder/Options from the Filter menu to open the Pathfinder Options dialog box. Enter a precision value to determine how precisely the Pathfinder filters will work, and if desired, select the Remove Redundant Points option or the Divide and Outline option to extract unpainted artwork after either the Divide or the Outline filter is used.

Pathfinder Options

Calculate results to a precision of 0.028 points   OK

☒ Remove redundant points   Cancel

☒ Divide and Outline will extract unpainted artwork   Defaults

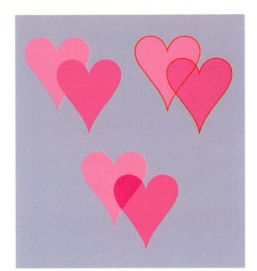

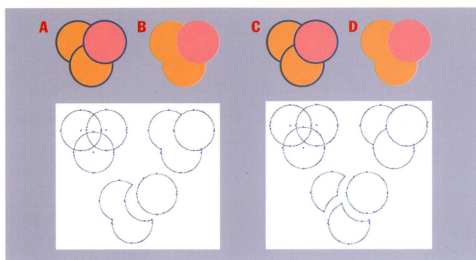

The Divide filter

This filter divides an image into its component *faces* or areas that are undivided by a line segment. We've added red outlines show how an image of 2 overlapped hearts was divided. We selected the inner shape and assigned a different colored fill to create a look of transparency.

The Outline filter

This filter divides an image into its component line segments or edges, which can then be selected individually or separated from each other. This filter is useful for creating specific path segments by overlapping 2 objects.

The Merge and Trim filters

The Merge filter removes any part of an object that is hidden behind another object, and merges any adjoining or overlapping objects that share the same fill color. The Trim filter works similarly to remove any part of an object that is hidden behind another, but does not merge

any adjoining or overlapping objects with the same color fill. We started with 3 overlapped circles (A, C) and applied the Merge (B) and Trim (D) filters. Black outlines below each example show the shapes of the 3 objects before and after use of the filter. The bottom figures separate the newly created parts of the filtered image.

The Crop filter

This filter excludes those parts of an image that fall outside the boundaries of the topmost object. To crop a Zapf Dingbats symbol converted to outlines, we drew and positioned a black square over it (A) and applied the Crop filter to crop the image into the square (B).

The Hard and Soft Filters

These filters create intermediate colors and use them to fill areas where objects of different colors overlap. The Hard filter combines 2 colors to represent how they will look when overprinted. It does this by creating a third object filled with a color using the highest values of the

CMYK components of the 2 original colors. So, for example, the blue triangle in our example is 50% cyan and 25% magenta, the purple triangle is 25% cyan and 50% magenta (A), and the overlapped area created by the filter is 50% of both cyan and magenta (B). The Soft filter creates a look of transparency. Enter a value of be-

tween 1 and 100 in the Soft dialog box to determine the mixing rate. We used 30% (C) and 100% (D) for this example, starting with the original blue and purple triangles. At a mixing rate of 100%, the cyan and magenta components of the original 2 colors were averaged to produce a hue of 37.5% cyan and 37.5% magenta.

17

Using the Polygon, Spiral, and Star Filters

Janet Ashford

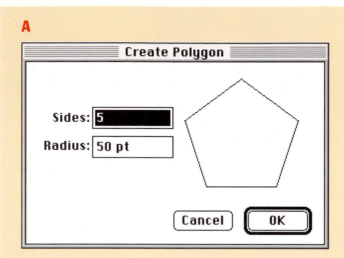

The Polygon, Spiral, and Star filters, all available under the Create submenu of the Filter menu, can be used to quickly create complex shapes that would be difficult or time-consuming to draw with the drawing tools.

A

Create Polygon

Sides: 5

Radius: 50 pt

Cancel   OK

B

Using the Polygon filter

The Polygon filter makes it possible to create a polygon with any number of sides and a specified radius in points. To create a polygon, choose Create from the Filters menu and Polygon from the submenu and enter values for number of Sides and Radius in the Create Polygon dialog box. A preview makes it possible to view the shape you have specified before clicking OK to create it (A). We used the Polygon filter to create a triangle, a diamond, a pentagram, a hexagon, a septegon, and an octagon by entering the numbers 3, 4, 5, 6, 7, and 8 respectively (B). The greater the number of sides in a polygon, the more it resembles a circle.

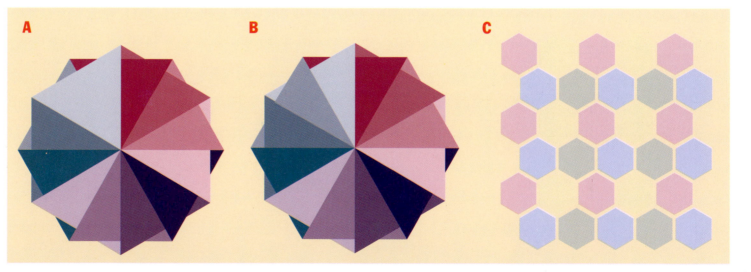

A   **B**   **C**

Using polygons

Polygons can be transformed and combined to create interesting designs and patterns. We created a triangle, copied it, and rotated the copies around a single point in 30° increments to create a starlike design. Each triangle was filled with a different color (A). We then used the pen tool to draw a small triangular patch shape to cover part of the last triangle, so that the design would look like an over-and-under series of overlapped shapes (B). We created a quiltlike pattern by creating a hexagon and copying it to create a row. We used the Align Objects filter to align the hexagons horizontally, then grouped them, copied the row, and used the Align Objects filter to align a grid of 6 rows vertically. During the process, we added colors to the hexagons (C).

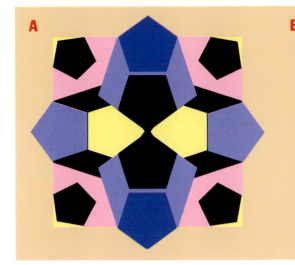

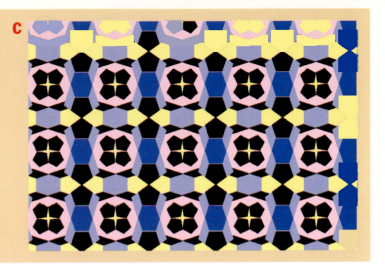

Creating a pattern fill

Polygons can be arranged to create designs that can be repeated to make a pattern fill. We began with pentagrams of various sizes and colors and arranged and overlapped them to create a symmetrical design (A). We drew a bounding rectangle around the design to define its boundaries as a tile. We then selected the rectangle and the design, opened the Pattern dialog box, and clicked New to create a new pattern. A preview of the pattern tile appears in the dialog box. We gave the pattern a name and clicked OK (B). Then we drew a rectangle and filled it with the pattern fill by choosing the Pattern icon in the Paint Style dialog box and clicking on the pattern name we wanted. The tile was automatically duplicated to fill the rectangle with a repeating pattern (C). ● *A bounding rectangle for a tile can be stroked and filled with None, simply to define the area of the tile, or with color, to create an additional background for the tile elements.*

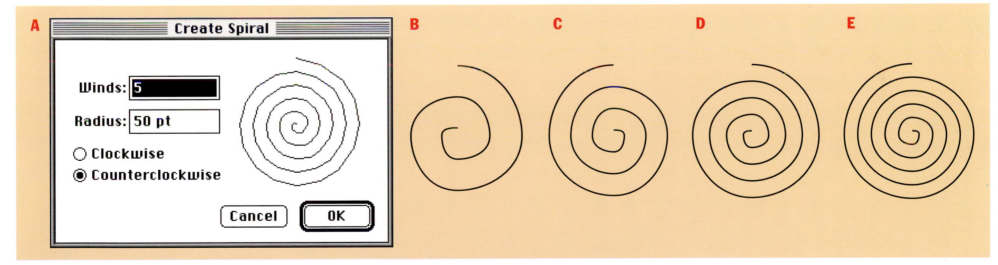

Using the Spiral filter

The Spiral filter makes it possible to create a spiral with any number of winds (complete turns around the center) and any radius. To create a spiral, choose Spiral from the Create submenu under the Filter menu to view the Create Spiral dialog box. Enter values for Winds and Radius and click on Clockwise or Counterclockwise to define the direction of the spiral from the center. A preview shows how the spiral will look (A). We created spirals with the following parameters: 2 winds, 50-point radius, counterclockwise (B); 3 winds, 50-point radius, clockwise (C); 4 winds, 50-point radius, counterclockwise (D); and 5 winds, 50-point radius, clockwise (E). Each of these spirals was given a 1-point black stroke and no fill.

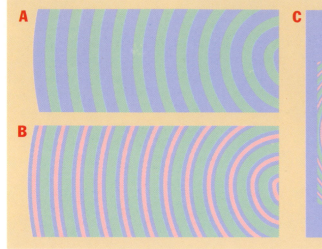

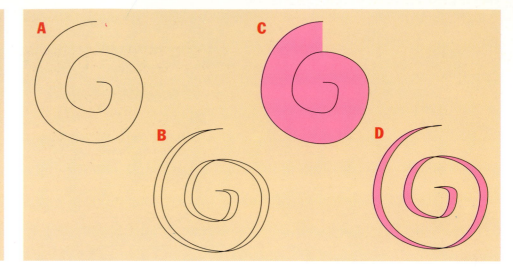

Adding stroke and fill to a spiral

Colored strokes and fills can be applied to a spiral to create an interesting pattern. We created a spiral with 12 winds and a radius of 200 points and gave it a green fill and a 9-point blue stroke, shown here in detail (A). We then used Copy and Paste In Front to paste a copy of the spiral directly on top of the original. We gave the copy a 3-point pink stroke and a fill of None to create a 3-color spiral design (B). We masked the round spiral inside a square and used it as a background in a book cover design. A large black-stroked spiral with only 2 winds was used as an additional decorative element (C).

Creating a ribbon

Ribbon spirals that look 3-dimensional can be created by overlapping and joining 2 identical spirals. We began with a 2-wind spiral (A), copied it, and positioned the copy to the right of the original (B). At this point, applying a fill to one of the spirals would fill its whole area (C). Instead, we used the direct-selection tool to select the 2 endpoints at the center of the 2 spirals, chose Join from the Object menu to join them, selected the 2 outer endpoints, and joined them to create a closed path that could be filled so that the color appears to be inside the ribbon shapes (D).

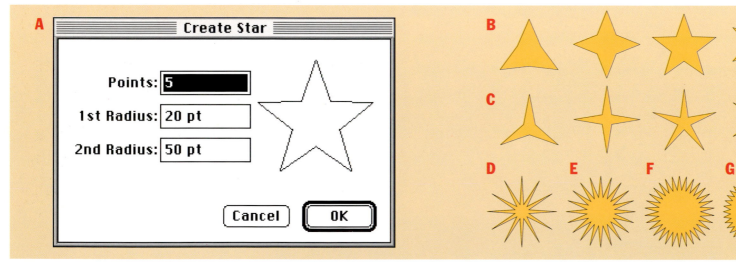

Using the Star filter

The Star filter is used to create star shapes with any number of points and with defined radii for the inner and outer points. To create a star, choose Star from the Create submenu under the Filter menu and enter the values you want in the Create Star dialog box. A preview shows how the star you have defined will look (A). We entered 20 points and 50 points for the 1st and 2nd radius values respectively and created stars with 3, 4, 5, 6, and 8 points (B). We then entered values of 10 and 50 points for the radii and created 3, 4, 5, 6, and 8-pointed stars with thinner points (C). By varying the distance between the inner and outer points you can create shapes which vary from starburst designs to circles with serrated edges. The stars shown here all have 12 points. Their 1st and 2nd radius values, in points, are 10, 50 (D), 20, 50 (E), 30, 50 (F), 40, 50 (G), and 45, 50 (H).

18

Designing Graphs

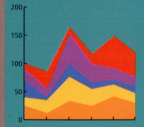

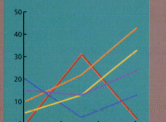

Graphic presentation of data attracts the reader's eye and piques curiosity about the information presented. But its main goal is to help the reader see important relationships in the information.

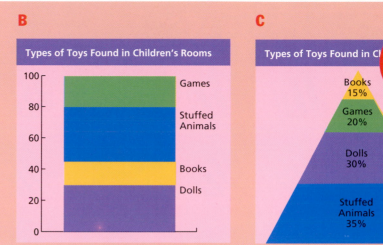

A Types of Toys Found in Children's Rooms

Dolls 30%
Games 20%
Books 15%
Stuffed Animals 35%

B Types of Toys Found in Children's Rooms

Games
Stuffed Animals
Books
Dolls

C Types of Toys Found in Children's Rooms

Books 15%
Games 20%
Dolls 30%
Stuffed Animals 35%

Choosing the right kind of graph

The goal of graphing is to achieve a clear and attractive portrayal of information. It's important to choose the right kind of graph for the data you want to present. A pie chart (available through the Graphs command in the Object menu) shows the relationship of parts to the whole (A). A variation is the single stacked bar (called a Stacked Column in Illustrator's Graph Style dialog box), with the data categories represented by "stripes" of differing thickness (B). The circular pie and the rectangular stacked bar work well for representing data, but other shapes are not appropriate. For instance, dividing a triangle into stripes is confusing because we are unsure whether to compare the heights of the stripes or their areas (C). In a 2-dimensional graph, area makes a stronger visual impact than height, but even if differences in area show the relationship, it's difficult to compare the size of the top triangle with that of a stripe lower down.

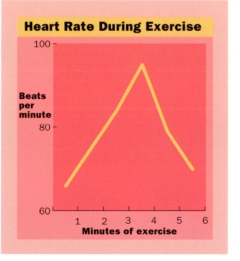

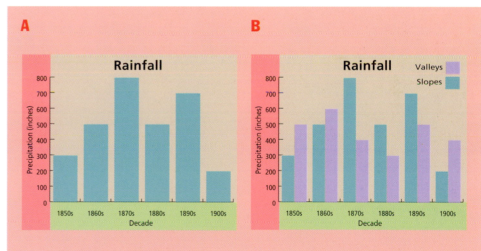

Data for graphs can be entered in Illustrator or imported from a spreadsheet application. A line chart (available through the Graphs command) is appropriate for showing the trend in changes in some measurement over time; the line that connects the data points gives a sense of motion from left (earlier data) to right (later data).

Histograms are good for comparing relative amounts or numbers of items that fall into a particular set of categories (A). To establish the number and width of bars in a histogram, you can either choose a desired "width" for the categories (such as a 10-year time period or a $5,000 salary range) and then use as many bars as you need to cover the range of the data; or you can choose a convenient number of classes and divide the range of the data by this number to arrive at the width of a bar. Illustrator's Grouped Columns histograms can also show how several kinds of data vary within a set of categories (B).

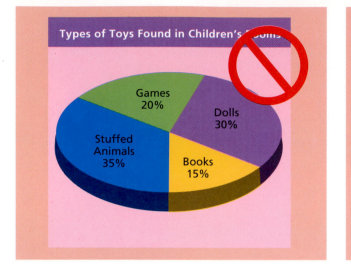

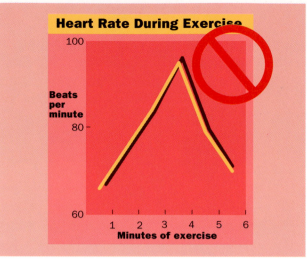

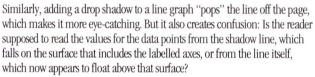

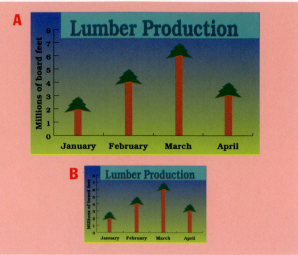

Modifying graphs

It's important not to distort graphs in the process of making them more visually appealing. Tilting a graph, for example, can make it more eye-catching, but can also distort the information presented; using the shear tool on a pie chart tends to make it harder for the reader to see the relationship between the sizes of the pieces of the pie.

Similarly, adding a drop shadow to a line graph "pops" the line off the page, which makes it more eye-catching. But it also creates confusion: Is the reader supposed to read the values for the data points from the shadow line, which falls on the surface that includes the labelled axes, or from the line itself, which now appears to float above that surface?

Using symbols in graphs

Another way to make a graph more appealing is to use spot illustrations as symbols for data points or for the bars in histograms. Symbols should be chosen carefully; their meaning should be obvious, as in using a tree to represent lumber production (A). They should also be simple, so that they will reduce well, maintaining their legibility at both large and small sizes (B).

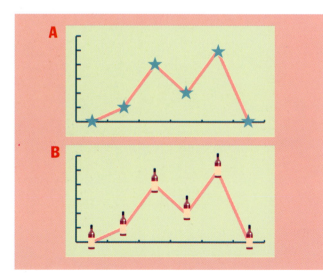

Symbols used as data points in a line chart or scatter graph should make it clear where the center of the data point is (A). A tall symbol (such as a wine bottle) is more likely to cause confusion about the location of the actual data point (B).

In histograms, you may intend the data to be represented by the *heights* of the symbols, but viewers tend to compare their *areas*. So, for instance, a wine bottle is not an ideal symbol. If you proportionally reduce it to make it half the height of another, instead of perceiving the 2:1 ratio of heights, the viewer perceives the area difference, more like a 4:1 ratio (A). If you reduce only the height, leaving the width the same, the result is better, but the ratio of the bottleneck to the

overall height of the bottle still creates confusion (B). Stacking symbols to form bars sometimes works better than using just 1 symbol per bar. Stacking bottles, however, results in narrow, precarious-looking bars (C). And when partial symbols have to be used, the difference in visual "weight" between the bottle top and bottom can cause confusion. For wine bottles, turning the symbol sideways before stacking creates wider, more stable histogram bars (D).

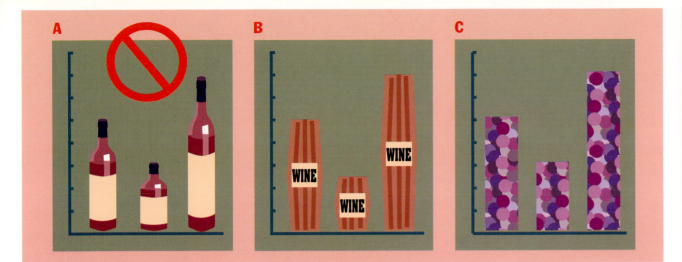

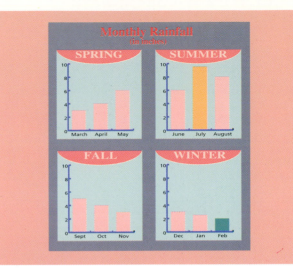

The height/area confusion caused by scaling symbols to make histogram bars (described at the bottom of page 54) can be made even worse if the symbols are made to look 3-dimensional, implying *volume* and making it hard to see where the top and bottom of the symbol are meant to be (A). Flat, stylized symbols like the bottles on page 54 tend to work better. Better yet, use shapes whose width is fairly consistent over their height (B), or use rectangular bars filled with a pattern made from a symbol (C).

Designing a series of graphs

A series of graphs can be used to compare similar data from different areas or time periods, for example. You can make it easy for the viewer to compare the graphs by making them identical in design (same size, colors, and so on), so that only the shifts in data draw attention. To highlight a particular part of the information, you can differentiate it with color or pattern.

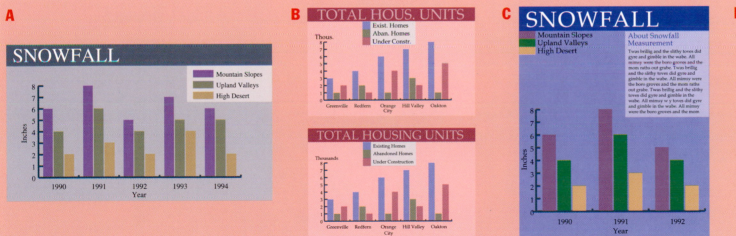

Using type with graphs

Type is used in graphs to label the axes and to add explanation. Here are some general tips for labeling graphs: In English and some other languages, using a horizontal rather than vertical graph design provides more room for text labels (A). In still other languages a vertical format may be more appropriate. Keep abbreviations to a minimum. By using fairly small type, which is

legible despite its size because there isn't very much text, you can gain the room needed to spell things out rather than abbreviating (B). Incorporate small blocks of information directly on the plotting field of the graph, if possible, rather than collecting these messages in a legend or putting them entirely in captions. That way the reader's eye doesn't have to jump from place to place on the page, interrupting the visual flow of the presentation (C).

Placing graphs near the text that refers to them more tightly integrates the text and graphs, strengthening the perceived connection between the information in the graph and that in the text (D).

19
Creating a Braided Medallion

Jim McConlogue, Warner Design Associates

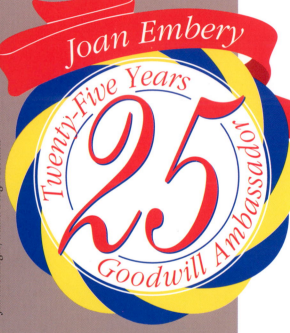

Illustrator's rotation tool makes it possible to create interesting designs by rotating shapes around a central point. This tool and the path-type tool were used to create a medallion for the San Diego Zoo's magazine, *ZooNooz*.

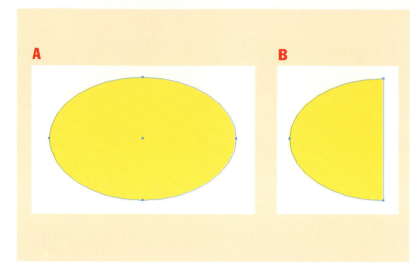
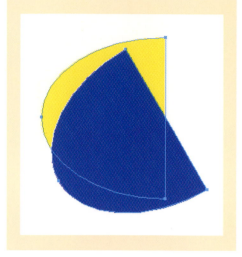

A   **B**

1 Creating a half-oval
To begin the blue and yellow braided pattern for the outside of the medallion, Jim McConlogue of Warner Design Associates in San Diego, first used the oval tool to draw a horizontal oval and filled it with a yellow custom color (A). He then used the scissors tool to cut the oval at its top and bottom anchor points and deleted the right half to create a half-oval shape (B).

2 Rotating the half-oval
McConlogue used Copy and Paste In Front to create a copy of the yellow half-oval exactly on top of the original and then clicked at the center of its straight edge with the rotate tool and entered a value of 30 degrees in the Rotate dialog box. He filled the rotated copy with blue.

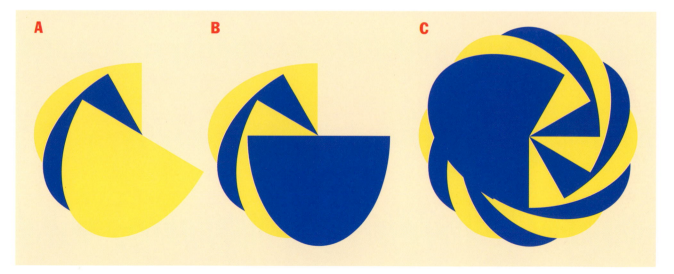

A   **B**   **C**

3 Using Repeat Transformation to complete the rotations
Using the same center point as a reference (the point where the 2 half-ovals crossed each other), McConlogue used the Copy, Paste In Front, and Repeat Transformation commands in sequence (Command-C, -F, -D) to continue copying and rotating half-ovals around the point (A, B), alternating the colors between yellow and blue until the ovals had come full circle (C).

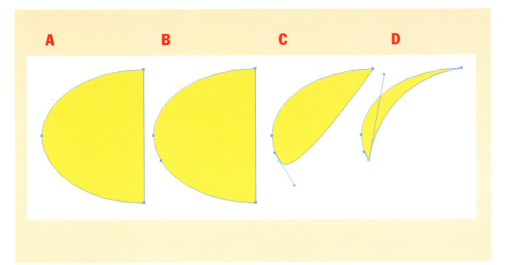

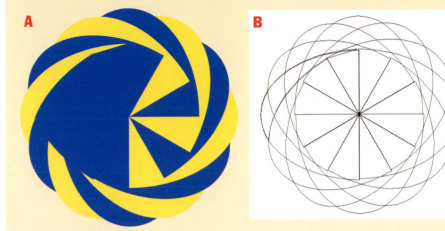

4 Creating a sliver

The edge of the first yellow half-oval, now at the bottom of the stack, was partially covered by the last blue half-oval to be rotated, so McConlogue needed to create a sliver shape to position on top of the design so that the braided edge would be correct. To do this he copied the original yellow half-oval (A), used the add-anchor-point tool to add a point just below its left center point (B), deleted the half-oval's bottom point (C), and then dragged the lower end of the direction line of the new point until the inside curve of the sliver assumed the shape he wanted (D).

5 Positioning the sliver

McConlogue positioned the yellow sliver on top of the original yellow half-oval and the last blue half-oval so that the look of a braided edge was completed (A). A look at the design in Artwork mode shows its symmetrical, mandala-like construction (B).

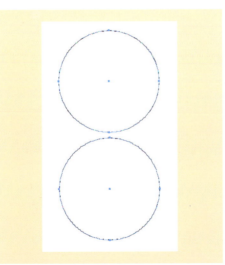

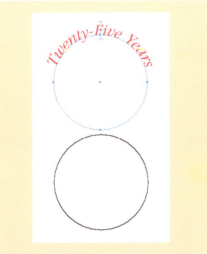

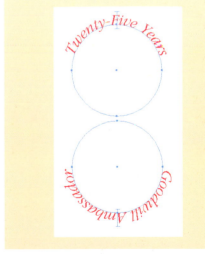

6 Adding a white circle

A white-filled circle was drawn and positioned in front of the design both to obscure the half-oval edges at the center of the braided elements and to provide a background for the curved type that was created next.

7 Creating type above and below a circle

To create type that curved around the top and bottom of the inner white circle McConlogue first created a pair of black circles that were slightly smaller than the white inner circle on the medallion. These were arranged one above the other.

8 Typing characters on the upper circle

McConlogue selected the top circle, then clicked with the path-type tool on its top center point, and typed characters in 17-point Garamond Light Italic with a Horizontal Scale of 90%, and then specified Centered alignment and a red color.

9 Typing characters on the lower circle

McConlogue clicked with the path-type tool on the lower circle's bottom anchor point and typed characters with the same type specifications onto the bottom of the bottom circle. The characters appeared upside-down at first.

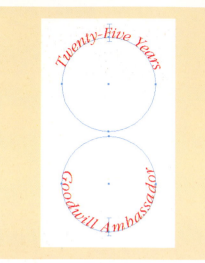

10 Flipping the lower type

To flip the lower type so that it appeared upright along the inside of the lower circle McConlogue used the selection tool to drag the lower I-beam upward. ⚫ *Flipping type at the bottom of a circle can also be done by double-clicking on the I-beam.*

11 Applying a baseline shift

To move the type below the baseline so that the tops of the characters were aligned to the bottom of the circle (A), McConlogue used the Character palette to apply a baseline shift of −11.5 points (B). ⚫ *If you do not know what point value to enter to raise or lower the type to the position you want, enter different values in the Baseline Shift field in the Character palette, press Return or Tab after each entry, and view the results until the baseline is shifted correctly.*

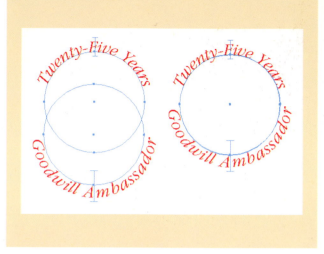

12 Overlapping the two circles

To create the look of type curved around a single circle, McConlogue moved the 2 circles until they were exactly on top of each other.

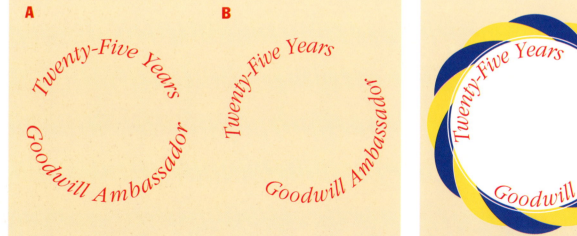

13 Rotating the curved type

McConlogue then selected the two circles with their type elements (A) and rotated them about 22 degrees to the left (B) by clicking on them with the rotate tool and dragging them to the position he wanted.

14 Positioning the type on the medallion

McConlogue added the rotated type to the center of the medallion and then added a decorative white line around the center white circle by copying it, pasting the copy in front of the original, scaling it up slightly from the center, and giving it a white stroke and no fill.

15 Adding larger numerals

McConlogue set the numerals "25" in Shelley Allegro Script (A), selected the type with the selection tool, and chose Create Outlines from the Type menu to convert the type characters to path outlines (B). He distorted the numerals by applying a horizontal scale of 90% and a vertical scale of 120%, filled the outlines with solid red and placed them at the center of the medallion (C).

16 Creating a drop shadow

To create a drop shadow for the numerals, McConlogue selected them and used the Copy and Paste In Back commands to paste a copy exactly behind the original. He changed the copy's fill to blue and used the selection tool to move it slightly down and to the right.

17 Finishing the medallion

The last step in finishing the medallion was to add a decorative blue line along the inside of the curved type. To create it McConlogue used the oval tool to draw a circle and gave it a blue stroke and no fill. He then used the add-anchor-points tool to add points to the circle, cut the circle into segments with the scissors tool, and deleted the unwanted portions.

18 Using the medallion in the magazine

The San Diego Zoo's magazine, *ZooNooz*, is produced in QuarkXPress. The designers at Warner Design Associates imported the medallion file into the XPress layout document and used it on the contents page and on 2 pages of an article about the 25th anniversary of the Zoo's Goodwill Ambassador, Joan Embery.

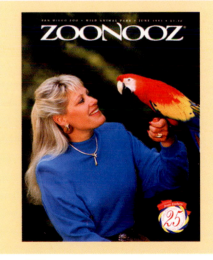

19 Creating a variation with a banner

McConlogue wanted to create a special version of the medallion featuring Joan Embery's name for the cover of the magazine. He used the pen tool to draw 4 banner shapes and filled 3 with bright red and one with a darker red (A). The shapes were layered both in front of and behind the medallion so that they look like a ribbon banner curling around it, with the darker red shape serving as a shadowed area. Two curved white lines completed the banner (B).

20 Setting and adjusting type on a curve

The type for "Joan Embery" was set in 18-point Garamond, reversed to white and typed with the path-type tool onto a curved path drawn along the bottom of the banner (A). McConlogue then entered a baseline shift of 5.5 points to raise the type until it was centered within the banner (B). ● *A shortcut for baseline shift is Option-Shift–up arrow (or down arrow).*

21 Using the medallions on the cover

The medallion with the banner was imported into the QuarkXPress magazine layout and positioned over a photograph of Joan Embery on the cover.

20

Rotating Elements for a Round Logo

Steve Musgrave

A round logo for a pharmaceutical company was created by using the rotate tool to position graphic letterforms around an arc, and to rotate triangle shapes to make a serrated circle and a starburst pattern.

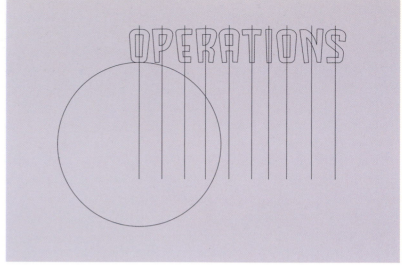

1 Drawing graphic letterforms
Illustrator's path-type tool can be used to fit typed letters to a curve. But custom lettering is sometimes constructed of drawn shapes, as in this design by Steve Musgrave, who used the pen tool to draw each letterform.

2 Lining up the letterforms
To fit these graphic letters to a curve for a round logo, Musgrave first used the Compound Paths command from the Object menu to combine each letterform with its counters (inner shapes) so that they would be transparent. He then grouped each letter with a guideline drawn through its center and positioned them at the top of a circle guide with the "O" in the 12 o'clock position.

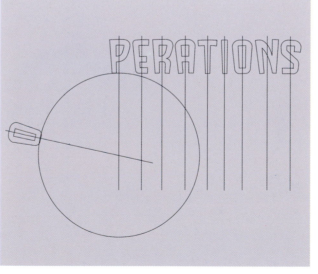

3 Rotating each letterform
Musgrave set the 0/0 point of Illustrator's ruler guides at the center of the circle guide, selected the letter "O" and its guideline, clicked at the center of the circle with the rotation tool, and dragged to rotate the "O" to the position he wanted. He then moved the "P" and other letters to the left.

4 Positioning the letterforms
He used the same procedure to rotate each of the letters, and then deleted their guidelines. He positioned the letters so that they were just touching, but let the "P" overlap the "E" and let the arms of the "T" overlap its neighbors slightly, to compensate for the wider spaces at the bases of these letters.

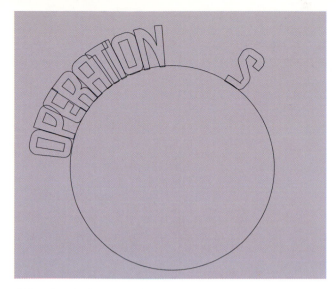

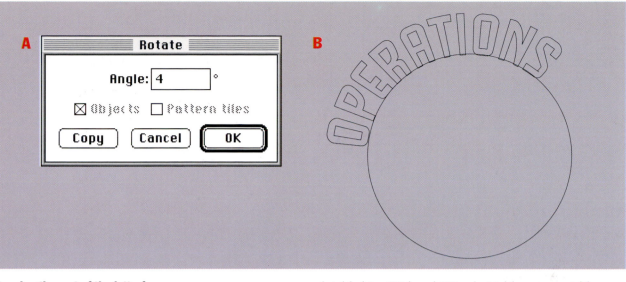

5 Spacing the last letterform

To space the letters evenly, Musgrave first used the rotate tool to move the last letter, the "S," along the curve to the position he wanted. He did this by using the center of the circle as a reference point, and dragging the mouse so that the "S" slid along the arc until it was in the right place.

6 Spacing the rest of the letterforms

Musgrave Option-clicked with the rotate tool to bring up the Rotate dialog box, which displayed the number of degrees the "S" had just been rotated. He divided this number by the number of spaces between the letters, to determine what size the angle between each pair of letters should be (A). He then selected the letters "P" through "N" and rotated them as a group 4 degrees around the circle's center. He deselected the "P" and rotated the rest of the group by 4 degrees. He repeated this procedure until all the letters were spaced along an arc. Because the "T" and "P" were already closer to their neighbors, rotating them 4 degrees produced the correct spacing (B).

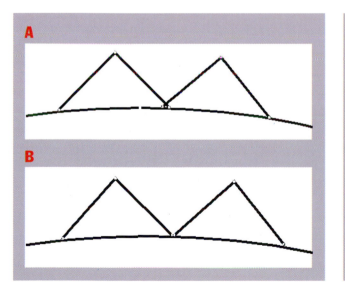

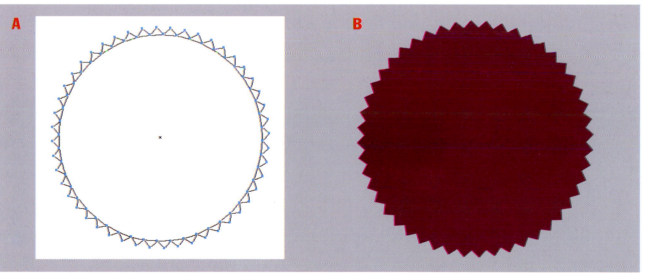

7 Creating a serrated circle

To create a serrated circle with 48 points, Musgrave drew a circle guide with a small angle at its edge. He copied the angle, pasted the copy in front, rotated it 7.5 degrees around the circle's center (A), moved the inner end points of the angles together to overlap them, and adjusted the angles (B).

8 Duplicating and joining the triangles

Musgrave copied the second angle, pasted it in front, and rotated the copy 7.5 degrees around the circle's center. He then typed Command-C, -F, -D (Copy, Paste In Front, and Repeat Transform) to repeat the copying and rotating until there were 48 triangle shapes around the circle, all with their end points overlapped (A). He deleted the circle guide, selected all the angles and used the Pathfinder, Unite filter to combine them into a single object, which he filled with dark brown (B). ● *A serrated circle can also be made by using the Star filter to create a multi-point star, as described in step 13.*

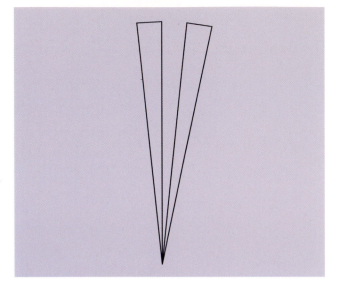

9 Combining the circle and letters

The letterforms on a curve were filled with orange and positioned over the brown circle background. Because the letterforms are compound paths, the inner shapes or "counters" are transparent and allow the brown background to show through.

10 Creating a starburst pattern

To create a starburst pattern, Musgrave first used the pen tool to draw a long thin triangle. He copied the triangle and pasted the copy in front and then used the rotate tool to rotate the copy 12 degrees, using the sharp point of the triangle as the center of rotation.

11 Rotating the triangles around the centerpoint

Musgrave typed Command-C, -F, and -D (Copy, Paste In Front, and Repeat Transform) to repeat the copying and rotation operations until he had produced a pattern of 30 evenly spaced triangles radiating from a single center point. He filled the triangles with blue.

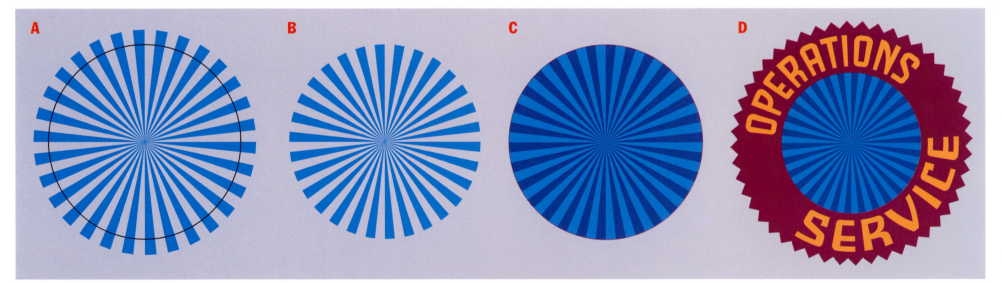

12 Masking the starburst pattern

To round off the outside edges of the triangles, Musgrave drew a circle slightly smaller than the starburst, and centered it in front of the starburst (A). He copied the circle to the clipboard and then selected the circle and the starburst and chose the Pathfinder, Crop filter to crop the starburst into the circle so that the outside edges of the starburst were clipped off (B). He then chose Paste In Back from the Edit menu to paste the circle copy in back of the clipped starburst and gave it a fill of dark blue and a black stroke (C). He placed the finished element at the center of the logo design (D).

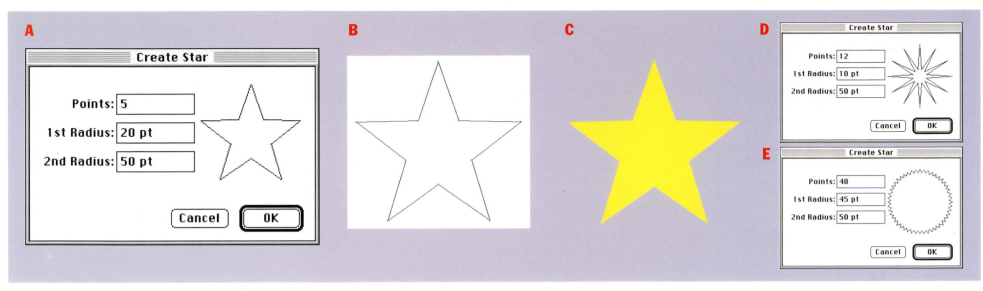

13 Using the Star filter

Musgrave created a star for the center of the logo. To create a star, choose Create from the Filter menu and Star from the submenu to bring up the Create Star dialog box, which allows you to specify the number of star points and the radius from the center of the star to its outermost points (1st Radius) and from the center to the inner points (2nd Radius). The default values produce a 5-pointed star. A preview within the dialog box shows how the star will look (A). To produce the star, shown here in Artwork mode (B), click OK. Musgrave filled his star with solid yellow (C). He then enlarged the star about 220 percent to fit the size of the logo. ⌘ *The shape of the preview star is up-dated as values in the Create Star dialog box are changed. Increasing the difference between the first and second radii produces deeper spikes (D), while reducing the difference produces shallower spikes. Using 48 points and shallow spikes creates a star like the serrated circle in step 8 (E).*

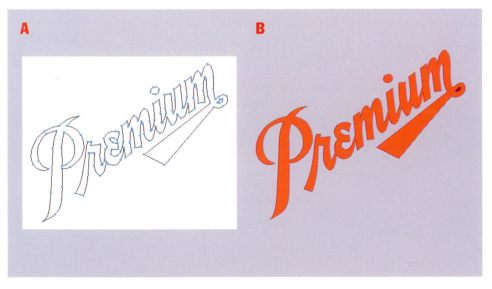

14 Creating script lettering

To create script-style lettering for the center of the logo, Musgrave made a pencil sketch based on lettering in an old typeface book. He scanned the sketch and autotraced the scan with Streamline. He then opened the autotracing in Illustrator (A). He selected the letterform shapes and specified a red fill and thin brown stroke (B).

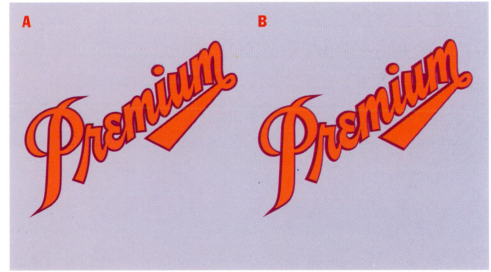

15 Adding a shadow

To add a dark brown shadow behind the red lettering, Musgrave used the Copy and Paste In Back commands to place a copy of the lettering directly behind the original and specified no fill and a thick brown stroke (A). He then moved the brown copy slightly to the left of the red original (B).

16 Modifying the star

With the lettering positioned over the star, Musgrave saw there was a gap between the right upper arm of the star and the tail of the lettering (A). So he selected the control points at the inner point and outer point of that arm and moved them down so that the yellow of the star filled the gap. He also drew a

shape to mask off the point of the "P." The strokes of the new shapes are shown here in black (B).

17 Finishing the design

The finished logo, assembled from 5 separate, overlapped parts, provides an interesting contrast between straight-edged and curving forms.

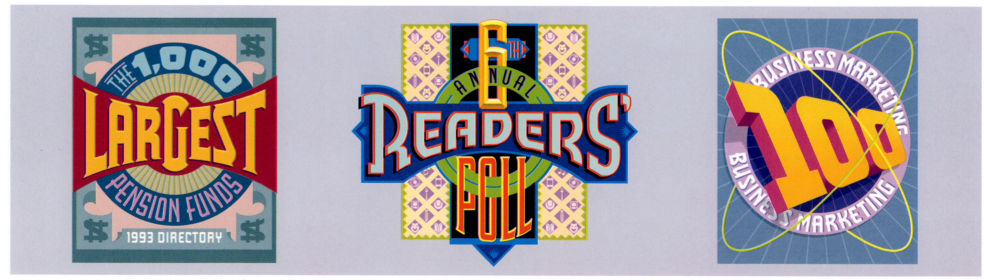

18 Creating other designs

Musgrave used similar techniques of placing type on a path and creating custom lettering to create these illustrations.

21

Creating a Resort Identity

Cabo del Sol

A brightly-colored logo mark and type were created and used at several sizes to provide graphics for the printed materials needed by a new resort in Mexico.

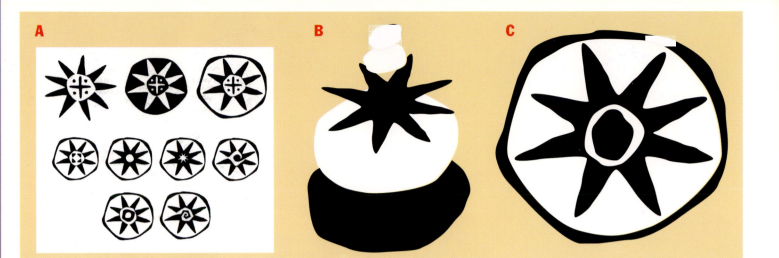

1 Creating a logo mark and type

To develop identity materials for a new golf and tennis resort at the tip of Baja California, the designers at CWA, Inc., under the direction of principal Susan Merritt, began by designing a logo mark and type. The mark features a sun symbol rendered in a hand-drawn style, to reflect both Mexico's sunny climate and its tradition of native hand-crafts, as well as the name of the resort, Cabo del Sol, which means Cape of the Sun. The designers made many rough sketches on paper, one of which is shown here (A). The final design was drawn directly in Illustrator, without a scanned template, and was rendered as a series of overlapping black and white shapes (shown here in an exploded view) (B). The first version of the logo mark was created in black-and-white (C).

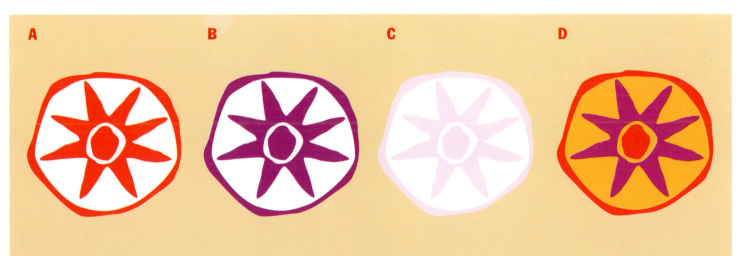

2 Creating color versions

To create the 1-color version that they planned to use for a press release sheet and envelope, the designers saved 3 versions of the original logo mark, changing the black shapes to red (A), purple (B), and a 10% screen of purple (C). They also created a 3-color version of the logo mark for use on the press folder, prospectus folder, maps, information sheets, and other materials. For the folders, Pantone colors were specified so that the files could be output as spot color separations for printing with PMS 185 (red), 247 (purple), and 1365 (deep yellow) (D). The Pantone colors were converted to process colors to create a second version of the logo mark for use on other printed pieces that were composed in Aldus PageMaker and that included color photographs requiring 4-color process printing. The CMYK specifications for the Pantone colors were estimated using a chart provided by the color separator.

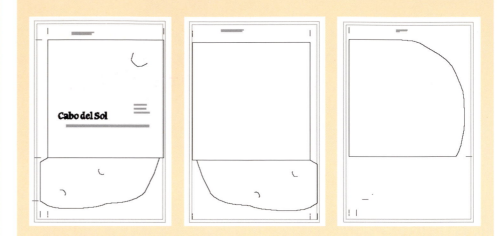

3 Creating type for the logo

To create the type for "Cabo del Sol" the designers first set type in Caxton (A). They kerned the type to create a more pleasing relation between characters and then used the Create Outlines command to convert the type to outlines so that the logo could be printed by any service bureau, regardless of whether they owned the Caxton font (B). The shapes were filled with purple (C) and positioned below the mark for a combined logo (D). The type was also saved as a separate document and used alone on some printed pieces or placed over large versions of the logo on the folders.

4 Preparing a die-cut guide

The logo mark and type were used on a 3-panel folder that encloses brochures and other materials. Because of the folder's large size (30 inches long x 14.5 inches tall when unfolded) the designers created a separate Illustrator file for each of the panels. The files include black-and-white line art to indicate the position of die-cut lines for the cover, pocket edges, slots for the insertion of business cards, and a flap used to close the folder. The cover and the inner pockets have irregular die-cut edges that were cut from an enlarged logo mark and adapted.

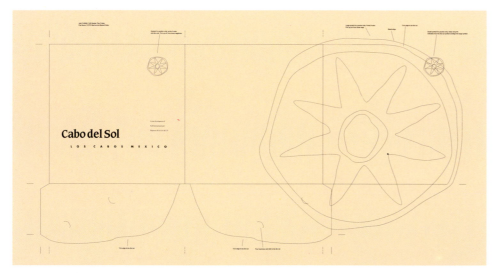

5 Creating a mechanical

The designers also created a black-and-white line art mechanical to serve as a guide for the printer for conventional stripping of the color art. The mechanical was supplied both as a laser print at a reduction and as negative film at 100%, output in pieces because the imagesetter could not handle the large size. The mechanical includes comments to guide the printer and indicates a bleed for the logo mark on the cover.

6 Ganging the color art

The logo mark and type at the correct sizes were ganged together in one document for output to spot color separations. The film was then stripped together conventionally by the printer, using the black-and-white mechanical as a guide.

7 Laying out the prospectus folder

Color comp versions of the mechanical show the placement of logo marks, type, and large areas of red and deep yellow color on the outer (A) and inner (B) sides of the prospectus folder. Black lines indicate the cutting and folding lines. The points along the right-hand side of the logo mark's outermost red shape were selected and pulled to the right slightly to provide a bleed. The folder was printed on a heavy, glossy white paper speckled with tones of red, yellow, and purple. The speckle was created conventionally by making a high-contrast negative of Speckeltone, a commercial paper, and printing it in red, yellow, and purple, with the 3 colors slightly offset from each other.

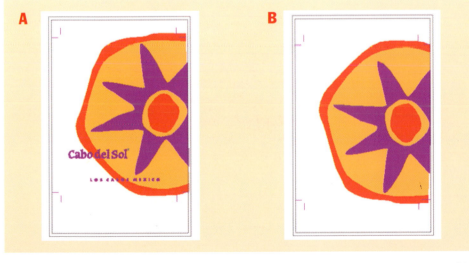

8 Creating a press folder

A more conventional 2-panel folder with straight-edged pockets was created to hold press releases for the resort. Screen dumps of the front (A) and back (B) covers show the placement of the type and logo mark. Rather than have the logo mark wrap across the front and back covers as with the prospectus folder, cropped versions of the logo mark were used in the same position on the front and back of the press folder. The folder was output to film in pieces, because of its large size, and the film was assembled conventionally. The printer created trapping where the type overlaps the enlarged logo mark.

9 Creating a press release and envelope

One-color versions of the logo mark and type, as well as screened type for the word "News," were created in Illustrator and imported into PageMaker for the layout of a press release sheet to be printed in red (A) and business envelope in purple (B). Additional type for the address and phone number of the resort was added in PageMaker. Versions of the 3-color logo were also imported into PageMaker layouts for a 2-sided information sheet and map.

Designing a Catalog Logo

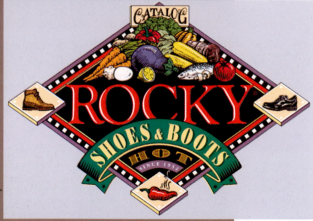

Designers from Eurostyle used custom type treatments, and scanned and autotraced spot illustrations to create a striking 4-color logo, and then adapted it to print 2- and 5-color versions.

A

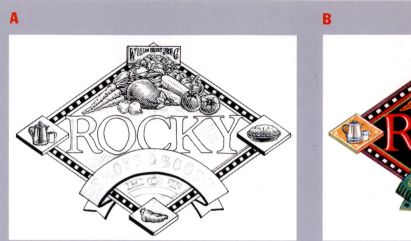

B

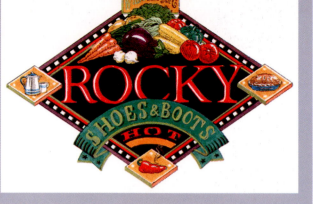

1 Creating a tight pencil sketch and a color comp

EuroStyle art director Ursula Sattler-Cohen designed a full-color logo for the front of a product catalog for Rocky Shoes & Boots, Inc. She used black pen and pencil to make a rough sketch (A) and then photocopied a final sketch onto translucent paper and added color with Berol Prismacolor markers (B). The concept for the catalog was to show full-color photo spreads of shoes and boots along with food items and recipes drawn from an employees' cookbook. To establish the link with food, illustrations of food items were incorporated into the catalog logo.

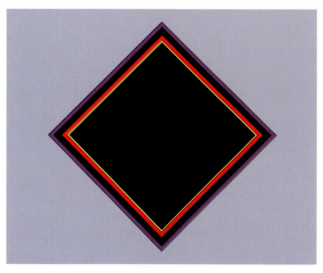

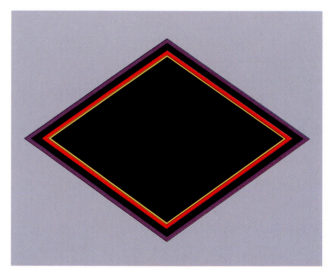

2 Drawing background shapes

The sketches were passed along to designer Claudia Braunwarth, who rendered the logo in electronic form. She began the background by drawing a square and rotating it 45 degrees. She filled it with black, copied the square, pasted the copy in front, scaled the copy uniformly, and changed the color. She repeated this sequence to create a pattern of 5 centered squares.

3 Applying a horizontal scale

Braunwarth then selected all the squares and applied a horizontal scale of 140% to stretch them horizontally into a diamond shape.

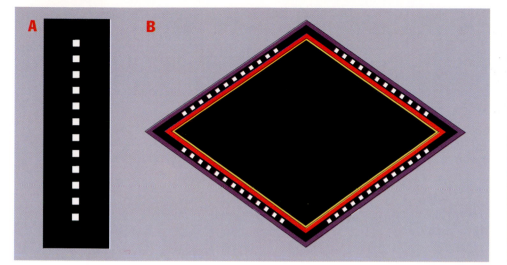

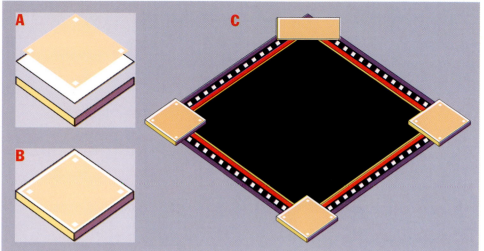

4 Adding decorative squares

To add a decorative border, Braunwarth drew a small white square, copied and pasted it in front, and moved the copy below the original. She then typed Command-C, -F, and -D (Copy, Paste in Front, Repeat Transform) to create a vertical row of 12 squares (A). She rotated the row –55 degrees and positioned it on the upper left edge of the background. She copied the rotated row, reflected the copy across the vertical axis, and positioned it on the right upper edge. Then she copied both rows, reflected the copies across the horizontal axis, and positioned them on the bottom edges of the background (B).

5 Creating corner elements

Corner elements were required as backgrounds for small illustrations. Braunwarth made them match the larger diamond-shaped background by copying the black inner diamond, scaling it down and changing its color to beige. She layered it over a white diamond with a black stroke, placed four small white diamonds on its corners, and added diagonal side pieces that made it look 3-dimensional. An exploded view (A) shows how the finished element (B) is constructed. Copies were placed on the side and bottom corners of the background, while a rectangular version was placed at the top (C).

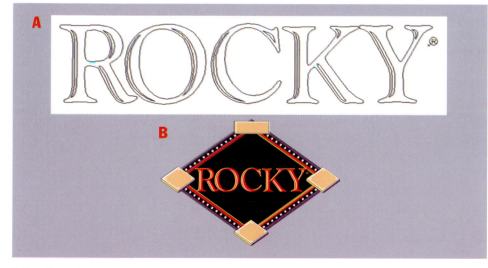

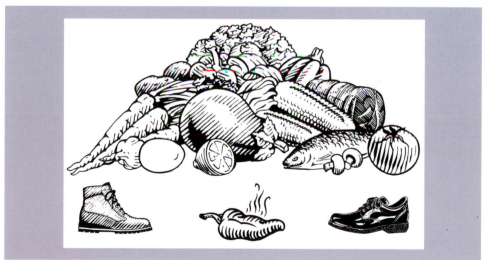

6 Creating a logotype

The Rocky company had already created a logotype of their name, based on the Goudy Hand-Tooled typeface. The designers scanned a copy of the logo, autotraced it with Adobe Streamline, and opened the autotracing in Illustrator. The logotype is shown here in Artwork mode (A). The letter shapes were filled with red, the highlights were filled with white, and the logotype was positioned in the center of the catalog logo (B).

7 Scanning and autotracing illustrations

Sattler-Cohen created 4 spot illustrations for the logo, using pen and paper. Her drawings were scanned and autotraced with Streamline, opened in Illustrator, and copied and pasted into the logo document.

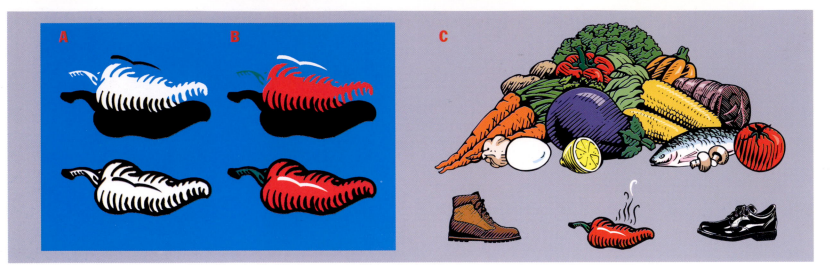

8 Adding color to the illustrations

The autotracing process rendered the line art by creating black- and white-filled shapes layered over each other, as with this chili pepper (A). To add color to the illustrations, Braunwarth selected each of the white elements and changed its fill to a color. In most cases the black shapes were left black, to serve as outlines. But the topmost stroke on the chili pepper was changed from black to white to create a highlight (B). Solid color fills were used for almost all of the shapes, though sometimes a gradient fill was used to add modeling, as for instance, on the fish in the large still-life (C).

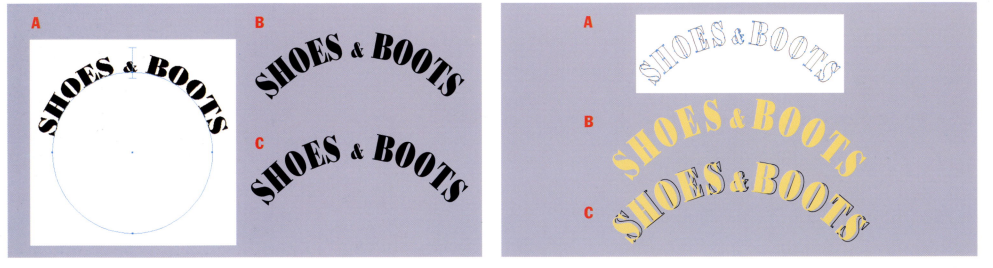

9 Setting type along a curved path

To set "Shoes & Boots" on a curve, Braunwarth drew a circle to create a path for the type and scaled it to fit over the bottom of the logo. She used the path-type tool to type the words along the circle (which then became invisible in Preview mode), specifying 58-point Bodoni Poster for the words, 34-point for the ampersand, and a Centered alignment (A). Braunwarth condensed the letters by applying a horizontal scale of 65% (B) and spread them by applying a Track of 40/1000 em (C).

10 Converting type to outlines

With the type selected, Braunwarth chose Create Outlines from the Type menu to convert the characters from type elements to graphic outlines, shown here selected in Artwork mode (A). She filled the outlines with a gold color (B), and then, to create a drop shadow, she typed Command-C, -B to place a copy of the outlines directly in back of the original. She specified a black stroke and a fill of None and then rotated the copy a clockwise, using the center of the original type's circle path as a reference point (C). ● *A circle used as a path for type, and its center point, are visible in Artwork mode.*

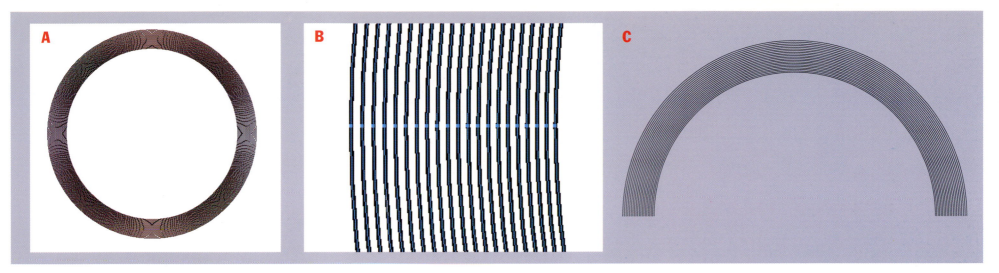

11 Creating concentric circles and arcs

To create a set of concentric arches that would provide a grating effect for the drop shadow for the "Shoes & Boots" type, Braunwarth first drew a circle with a black stroke, typed Command-C, -F to copy and paste it in front, then chose the Scale tool, held down the Option key, and clicked on the center of the circle to establish a reference point. She entered a uniform scale of 101%, unchecked the Scale Line Weight box, and clicked OK to enlarge the circle copy slightly from its center. She continued to type Command-C, -F, and -D (Repeat Transform) to create more circles until she had a pattern of 21 concentric circles (A). When the pattern of circles was completed, Braunwarth selected them all and used the scissors tool to cut the two side points of each of the circles. A close-up shows all the left-hand side points selected (B). She then selected and deleted the bottom half of each of the circles, to create a pattern of 21 concentric arcs (C). *Another way to cut the concentric circles in half is to draw a rectangle that covers the lower half of the circles, select both rectangle and circles, and choose Divide from the Pathfinder submenu under the Filter menu to cut all the circles at once.*

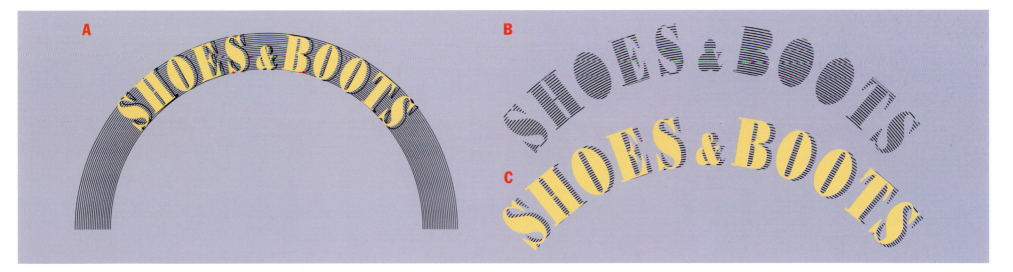

12 Masking the arcs into the drop shadow

To mask the arcs into the drop shadows, Braunwarth grouped the arcs and positioned them over the type (A). She then selected the drop shadow outlines and chose Compound Paths, Release from the Object menu to release the inner counter shapes from the outer shapes of the letters. She then selected only the outer outlines and chose Compound Paths, Make to combine these shapes into a new compound path. She selected this path and the arcs and chose Masks, Make from the Object menu to mask the arcs into the drop shadow outlines. The finished drop shadow is shown here alone (B), and in place behind the gold letters (C). *Either a single path or a compound path can be used as a masking object. However, using a compound path as a mask may cause printing problems.*

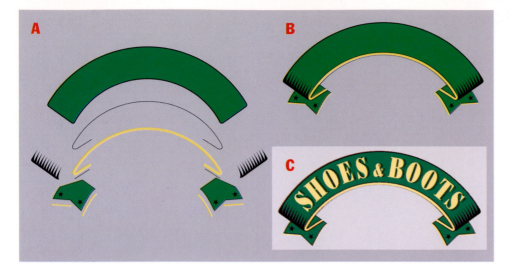

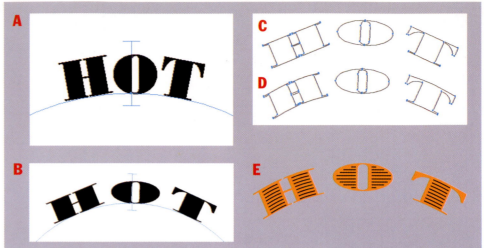

13 Constructing a banner

To create a green banner background for the gold type, Braunwarth used segments of concentric circles, and other shapes drawn with the pen tool to construct a graphic that looks like a folded banner with a gold edge and black details. An exploded view (A) shows the parts of the completed banner (B). The black stars are characters from the Zapf Dingbats font. The finished "Shoes & Boots" type was positioned over the banner (C).

14 Expanding PostScript type

To create a custom treatment for the word "Hot," Braunwarth used the path-type tool to set type in 30-point Bodoni Poster (A), using a circle that fit concentrically inside the circle she had used to set the type for the words "Shoes & Boots." She expanded the letters by applying a horizontal scale of 200% and applied a track of 120/1000 em to spread them (B). She then converted the letters to font outlines (C) and manipulated the anchor points to thicken the serifs and curve the tops of the letters (D). She filled the letter shapes with gold and drew short black decorative lines over them (E).

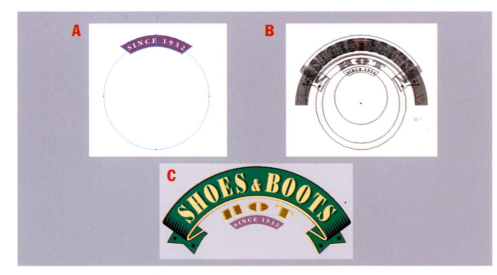

15 Finishing the curved type elements

To finish the type for the logo, Braunwarth drew another circle inside the circle used for setting the word "Hot" and set reverse type in Garamond. She used the pen tool to draw a background shape around the type and filled it with purple (A). An Artwork view shows Braunwarth's positioning of the circle paths for all the curved type (B). Though not exactly concentric, the baselines and heights of the 3 curved lines of lettering and their background shapes fit together in pleasing arcs (C).

16 Scanning hand-drawn type

Type for the word "Catalog" was drawn by hand by Sattler-Cohen. Her pen drawing was scanned, autotraced in Streamline, and opened in Illustrator. An Artwork view of the selected lettering shows the anchor points that define the curves and lines of the letters (A). The large letterforms were filled with black, and the counters (the shapes that define the interior spaces in the letters "C," "A," "O," and "G," were filled with the same beige used in the logo's corner pieces (B) so that when the lettering was positioned in the corner piece, the counters appeared to be transparent (C).

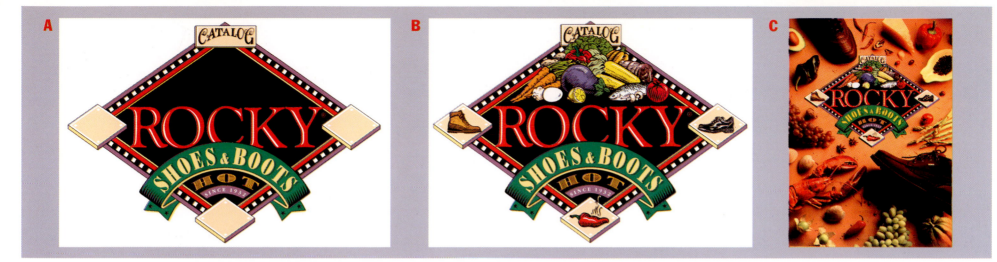

17 Finishing the logo and catalog cover

The finished type elements were positioned over the logo background (A). The spot illustrations were copied and pasted from separate files into the final logo file, scaled to fit, and positioned (B). For final output, the 4-color gold used for on-screen display and proofs was changed to a spot color so that a metallic ink could be used. The logo document was output as 5 pieces of film and stripped into the film for a conventionally separated photograph for the product catalog cover (C).

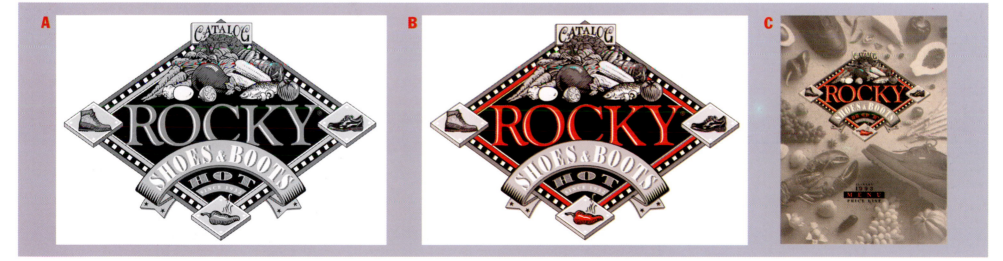

18 Creating a 2-color version

A copy of the 4-color logo was saved as a new document, and Braunwarth changed all the colors to tints of black, trying to match the tonal values of the original colors (A). She then changed the Rocky logotype and some other elements to red for use on a 2-color price list cover (B). The 2-color logo and additional type elements in black and red were output to film and stripped into the film for a black-and-white photograph for the cover (C).

Designing a Radio Station Identity

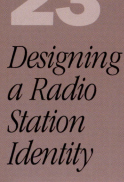

Bert Wahlen, General Manager

625 Broadway Avenue, Suite 1200

San Diego, California 92101

(619) 238-1037

fax (619) 238-1041

CWA, Inc.

A carefully crafted type treatment and simple starburst elements were applied to create 2 versions of a 2-color logo for a radio station, used on a variety of printed materials.

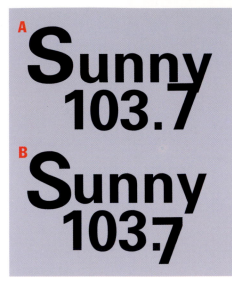

1 Setting type
To create a new logo for "Sunny 103.7," a San Diego radio station, designers at CWA, Inc., under the direction of principal Calvin Woo, set the station's name in 170-point Univers Bold.

2 Positioning 2 lines of type
To experiment with spacing, the name was retyped as 2 separate elements, and the lower line was raised. The designers saw that they would have to deal with the descender of the "y" overlapping the "7."

3 Arranging the type
The "S" was enlarged to 250 points and the "7" was enlarged to 200 points (A). Then these 2 characters were separated as independent type elements so they could be easily repositioned (B).

4 Finishing the logotype
The designers liked the Univers type overall, but wanted a more refined numeral "1." So they deleted the Univers character, typed a new "1" in Helvetica Bold, converted it to outlines, and edited it to thicken the stem. They also deleted the square-shaped Univers period and substituted a circle drawn with the circle tool (A). A view in Artwork mode shows the combination of type and graphic objects that made it easier for the designers to experiment with size and placement of elements (B).

5 Adding a color stroke and fill
To create a color version of the logotype, the designers selected all the elements and used the Paint Style dialog to specify a fill of PMS 313 (turquoise) and a 10-point stroke in PMS 116 (yellow).

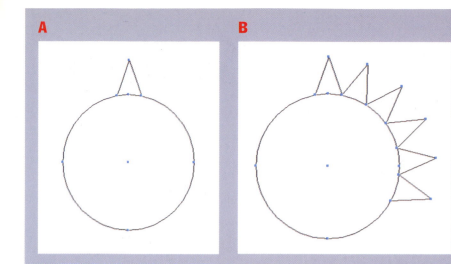

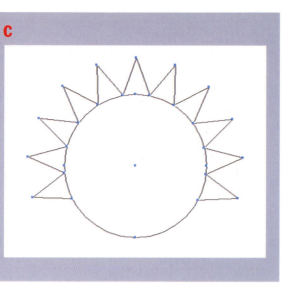

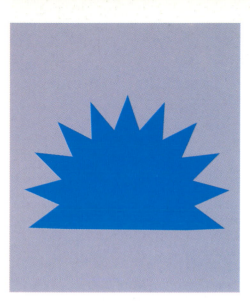

6 Creating a sun symbol

To create a graphic to reinforce the word "sunny," the designers first drew a circle (shown in Artwork mode), then drew 1 angled line at the top of it, and copied and flipped the line to create a symmetrical angle (A). The angle at the top of the circle was copied and pasted in front. Then, with the center of the circle as the center of rotation, the copy was rotated clockwise until its left end point overlapped its neighbor's right end point. The designers typed Command-C, -F, and -D (Copy, Paste In Front, and Repeat Transform) to repeat these operations until they had 6 angles (B). They then copied the lower 5 angles, pasted them in front, and used the reflect tool to flip the copies across the vertical axis of the circle (C).

7 Joining the angles

To join the angles into a single shape, the designers selected each pair of overlapping end points and chose Join from the Object menu, until they had created a single half-sun shape. They filled it with PMS 313.

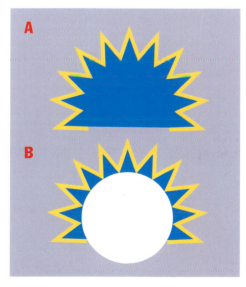

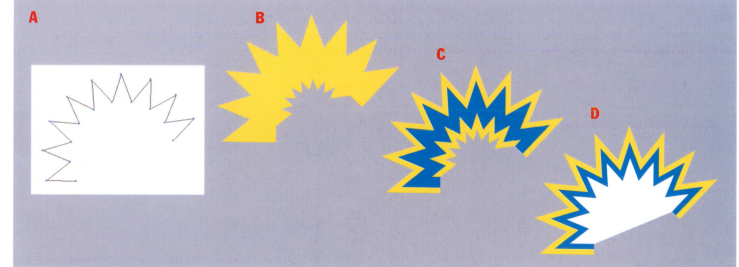

8 Adding a border and masking

The designers added a 10-point yellow stroke to match the strokes on the type (A), then masked off the interior of the symbol by giving the guide circle, which they had left in place, a white fill and no stroke (B).

9 Creating a sun symbol variation

To create a second version in which the sun shape has a zigzagged inside edge, the designers copied the original sun shape, used the scissors tool to cut away the 2 outermost angle elements, and then rotated the shape about 23 degrees counterclockwise (A). They gave the new path a 40-point yellow stroke and no fill (B), then copied it, pasted the copy in front, and gave the copy a 20-point blue stroke (C). Finally they pasted another copy in front and gave it a white fill and no stroke (D).

A

B

10 Positioning the logo elements

The first sun symbol was rotated −108 degrees and positioned on the right side of the logotype. The letters "FM" were set in 47-point Univers Bold and positioned inside the sun symbol. Then the second sun symbol was enlarged and positioned behind the "S" (A). When all the elements were in place, the entire logo was rotated by 22.5 degrees (B). (The objects with a white fill are visible when shown over a colored background in figure A but become part of the background when the art is printed on white paper as in figure B.)

11 Creating a tint version

To create a screened version of the logo as a variation, the designers selected the objects filled with turquoise and changed the tint setting in the Paint Style dialog box to 10%. They selected the yellow-filled objects and changed the tint percentage to 20%, because yellow is a lighter color than turquoise.

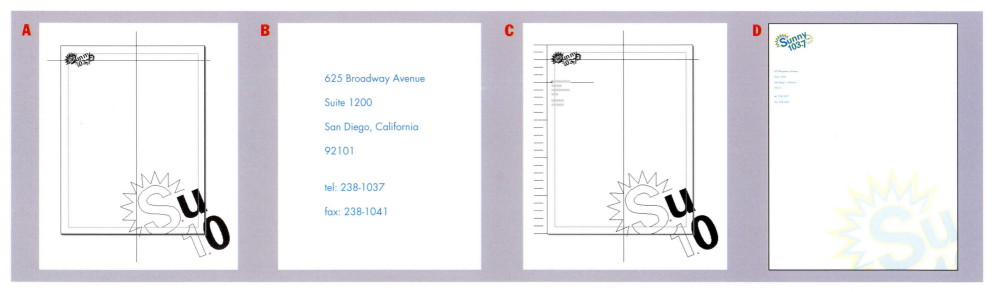

A

B

625 Broadway Avenue

Suite 1200

San Diego, California

92101

tel: 238-1037

fax: 238-1041

C

D

12 Using the logo on a letterhead sheet

To create a letter sheet, the designers set up an 8.5 x 11-inch page and pasted a copy of the finished logo into it. They scaled the logo down to a height of about 1 inch and positioned it at the top left corner of the page. They then pasted in a copy of the tint version of the logo, positioned it so that it over- lapped the bottom right corner of the page, and deleted unnecessary elements. A view in Artwork mode shows these elements in place (A). They then set the address and telephone numbers of the radio station in 7.5/9-point turquoise Futura Book, double-spaced, and positioned them below the small logo (B). To create a pleasing spacing of these elements, the designers divided the pages vertically by placing nonprinting guidelines at equal intervals along the edge of the page and positioned the top of the type block at one of the marks. A view in Artwork mode shows the guidelines (C). The finished sheet was output as spot color separations and printed in 2 colors (D).

13 Finishing the letterhead system

The 2-color logo and the tint version of the logo were combined in different ways on other materials to round out the letterhead set. For the business-size envelope, a single line of turquoise type set in 7.5-point Futura Book was used for the address line (A). For a business card, the address and telephone numbers were set in 6/7.5-point Futura Book, double-spaced, while the staff person's name was set in the same size in Futura Bold (B). The radio station also requested a lapel button, for which the 2-color logo was placed within a white circle (C).

14 Using the logo in advertisements

To create a 3.25 x 15.5-inch, 3-color bus poster, the designers converted the slanted logo from yellow and turquoise to yellow and white so they could use the turquoise to create a brightly colored background. They also created a red starburst shape by copying the sun symbol, adding angle shapes, and filling it with PMS 485. Additional type was set in white Univers Bold and rotated to match the tilt of the logo (A). For a magazine ad the logo was positioned over a background containing a blend from white down to 100% turquoise. Again, additional type was set in Univers Bold and rotated, along with yellow accent rules, to match the tilt of the logo (B).

EuroStyle

Using bold colors, simple shapes, and custom type treatments, EuroStyle produced a lively, colorful package label in 2 formats for a line of children's party favors.

1 Working with pre-existing elements

Designers at EuroStyle produced 2 new package labels by separating and re-combining elements taken from their first package design for the same client, created at their request by free-lance designer Mary Adsit (A). Important elements of the labels included the company logo, created in-house by EuroStyle (B), and a seal (C) and decorative headline type (D) designed and produced by Adsit in Aldus FreeHand. EuroStyle's designers converted the FreeHand elements to Illustrator format to begin the new package labels. In most cases some of the colors of the original elements were changed to fit the palette of the new labels.

2 Creating a checkerboard pattern

To create a checkerboard pattern like that used on the sides of Adsit's original design, EuroStyle designer Michele Davison began by using the rectangle tool with the Shift key held down to draw 1 black square. She used the Copy and Paste In Front commands to create a copy on top of the original and moved it to the right by the same distance as the width of the square. She used the Copy, Paste In Front, and Repeat Transform commands to repeat the copying and moving operations until she had a row of 9 evenly spaced squares (A). She selected all the squares, copied them, and positioned the copies below the original row, offsetting them so that the 2 rows of black squares were touching at their corners (B). She then copied both rows of squares and positioned the copies below the originals to create a 4-row pattern (C).

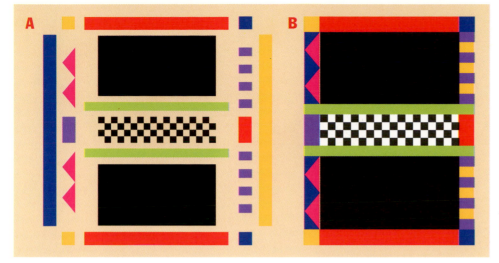

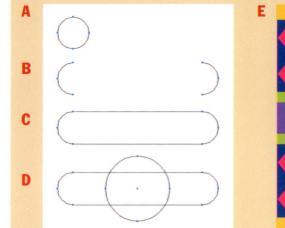

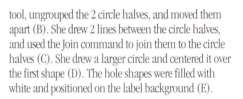

3 Assembling the background

Starting with the smaller of the 2 package labels, Davison used the rectangle and pen tools to draw a variety of additional geometric elements for the package label background, including rectangles, squares, and triangles. Each shape was filled with 1 of 6 bright colors or black (A). A white rectangle background was positioned behind the checkerboard and then all the elements were overlapped or positioned next to each other to fit the package dimensions, creating a symmetrical design that could be folded in half along the horizontal axis (B).

4 Creating and positioning die-cut shapes

The printed package includes a die-cut hole that fits over a retail rack. Davison created a hole-shaped marker to make sure important elements were not positioned where the package would be die-cut. She drew a small circle (A), cut its top and bottom points with the scissors tool, ungrouped the 2 circle halves, and moved them apart (B). She drew 2 lines between the circle halves, and used the Join command to join them to the circle halves (C). She drew a larger circle and centered it over the first shape (D). The hole shapes were filled with white and positioned on the label background (E).

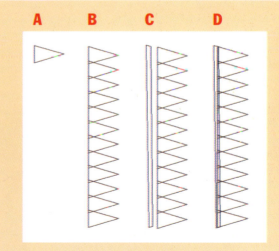

5 Editing type

To create a custom headline treatment like that designed by Adsit, you can start by setting the word "Party" in 76-point Lithos Black (A). Apply a Horizontal Scale of 90% (B) and then convert the type to path outlines using the Create Outlines command (C). Move each letterform individually to achieve the letterspacing shown (D).

6 Adding color and a drop shadow

To adapt Adsit's headline, Davison filled each letter with a different color (A). To create a drop shadow, group and copy the letters and fill the copies with blue (B). Position the blue set of letters behind the multi-colored set with an offset of a few points down and to the right (C).

7 Creating a decorative zigzag shape

To create zigzags, draw a triangle (A) and use Copy and Paste In Front to place a copy over the original. Move the copy down and then use Copy, Paste In Front, and Repeat Transform to create a row of evenly spaced, slightly overlapping triangles (B). Draw a thin, vertical rectangle (C) and position it alongside the triangles to cover their overlapping edges (D).

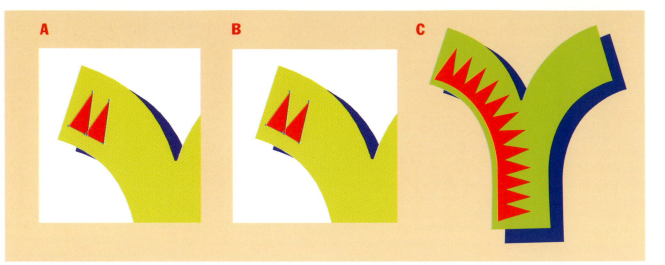

A   B   C

8 Adding the zigzags to the letters

Davison filled the zigzag shape with purple and positioned it over the red letter "P." She then made 2 copies of it, filled them with green and yellow, and positioned them over the "R" and "T." She made another copy, filled it with pink, and rotated it to match the angle of the "A." A special curved zigzag was made for the "Y."

9 Creating a curved zigzag

To create a curved zigzag shape for the letter "Y," you can copy a single triangle from the original zigzag shape and rotated it to match the curve at the top of the "Y." Copy the triangle and moved it to the right so that it just touches the original (A). Then use the rotate tool to rotate the second triangle a few degrees to follow the curve of the "Y," using the point where the two triangles touch as the reference point for the rotation (B). Continue the process of copying, moving, and rotating triangles until you reach the bottom of the "Y" and then use the pen tool to draw a thin, curving shape to cover the straight edges of the triangles (C).

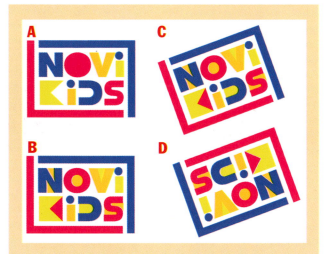

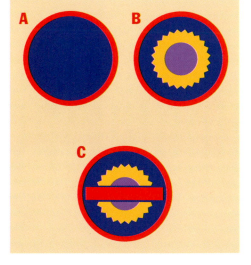

10 Creating a logo sticker

EuroStyle designer Ursula Sattler-Cohen designed a logo and designer Glen Cohen produced it in Illustrator using simple shapes to create the type (A) and adding contrasting color backgrounds and counters (B). Davison rotated the logo 20 degrees for use on the label front C). She copied the rotated logo and rotated the copy 180 degrees for use on the label back (D).

11 Finishing the label front

Davison positioned the headline type and logo sticker over the bottom half of the label background, which would be the label front when folded. She then added reverse type in 9.5/9-point Lithos Bold with a Horizontal Scale of 95%. She added a number of dots in different colors, which were made by typing a solid circle in the Zapf Dingbats font, copying it, and changing the colors.

12 Creating a decorative seal

To create a seal like the one Adsit created for the original box, you can first drew 2 concentric circles in contrasting colors (A). Next use the Star filter to create a serrated circle and add an inner circle (B). Draw nested rectangles over the center of the seal (C).

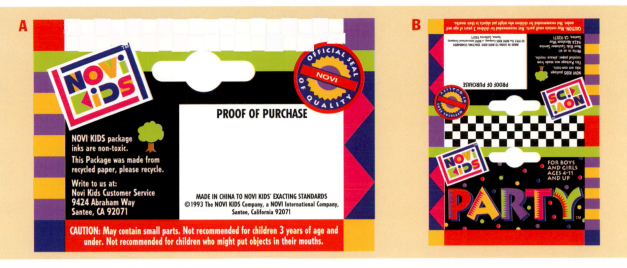

13 Adding type to the seal

White type was set over the center of the seal in 5-point Helvetica Bold with a Horizontal Scale of 158% and a Track of −10. White type was set on a circle path using 5.4-point Lithos Black, using the Paragraph dialog box to specify letterspacing of 72% for the type above and 218% for that below (A). The seal was then rotated −18 degrees (B).

14 Finishing the label back

The logo sticker, seal, and a simply drawn tree were positioned on the back of the label, along with a white rectangle to define a "Proof of Purchase" area and additional lettering set in Tempo Condensed Heavy in both black and white (A). All of these type and graphic elements were rotated 180 degrees so that they appeared upside down at the top of the completed label (B) and would appear right-side-up when the label was folded over the package.

15 Adapting the label to a different format

The same elements used on the small label, which measures 4.125 inches wide x 5.5 inches deep, were adapted to fit a larger label format that measures 7.3125 inches wide x 5.5 inches deep. The border elements were moved outward to fit the new width and the interior black rectangles were enlarged to fill the new space. Additional decorative colored dots were added to the la-

bel front along with new decorative green diamond shapes on the bottom border (A). Additional type set in both Lithos and Tempo Condensed was added to the label back (B).

25

Developing a Corporate Logo

Jack Davis and Jill Davis

Illustrator's drawing and color capabilities make it possible to develop a variety of logo variations for client approval, then refine the final choice to create finished corporate identity materials.

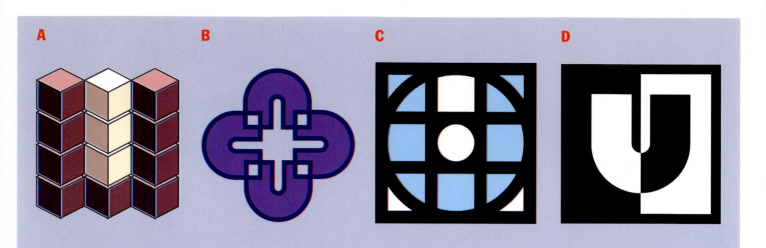

1 Exploring alternatives

University Associates, a developer of business and shopping plazas, wanted a 2-color logo that projected the image of a "corporate" (solid, well-established) yet forward-thinking firm. At the beginning of the logo design process, their only other criterion was that the mark include the initial "U" in some form. The Davis design team started by exploring an architectural ap-

proach (A), a rounded mall tile look (B), a square approach that combined the architectural and tile directions (C), and an approach based on an obvious use of the letter "U" (D).

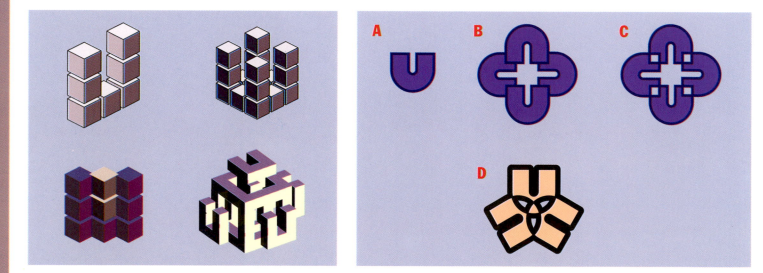

2 Exploring the architectural approach

Jack Davis began by creating several constructions of cubes in a 3D program, saving them in EPS format, and opening them in Illustrator, where he selected the various faces and assigned strokes and fills with the Paint Style palette. Each construction incorporated a built-up letter "U" in some form.

3 Developing rounded marks

To create a rounded mark, the designers converted a typeset "U" to font outlines (A) and then rotated it in 90-degree increments around a reference point just above the "U" (B). They then used the Exclude filter (from Filter, Pathfinder) to create "holes" where the letterforms overlapped (C). A variation was created by copying the outline and rotating it twice in 120-degree steps around the base of the "U" (D).

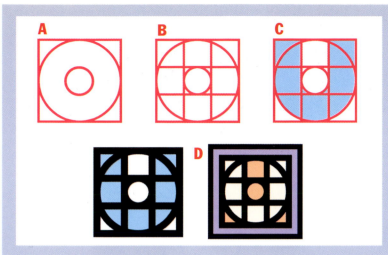

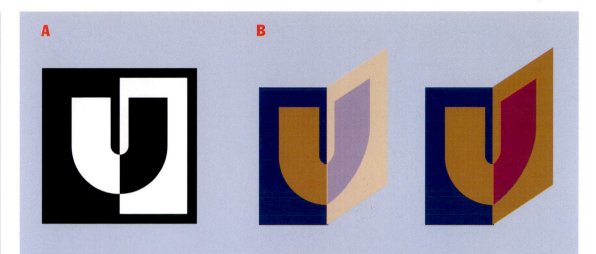

4 Developing the square option

Jack Davis drew the "U" for the next approach by placing 2 circles inside a square (A) and then dividing the square into 9 smaller squares using vertical and horizontal lines (B), creating a play between the graceful curves of the circle and the solid, stable squares. He emphasized the shape of the "U" by adding color to the areas that define it (C) and created different colored versions both with and without borders (D).

5 Focusing on the letter

The designers tried an approach in which the letter "U" was the only prominent feature. To build the negative-positive interaction, they converted a typeset "U" to outlines and used the scissors tool to cut it in half vertically. They filled one half with white, the other with black, and drew rectangles with contrasting fills behind them (A). Then, to create a variation, they added color, selected the rectangle and "U" half on the right, and used the shear tool to create a 3-dimensional effect (B).

6 Eliminating some of the approaches

To help the client decide, the designers placed each of the 4 candidate logo marks in a business card layout, setting sample type in several different fonts. Then, through a narrowing process that involved several steps, the designers and client chose the square approach and developed it further. They rejected the negative-positive "U" approach as the weakest of the 4 design directions (A). The architectural option was eliminated because the plazas that University Associates develops are all single-storey constructions (B). The rounded marks were considered decorative but not "corporate" enough (C).

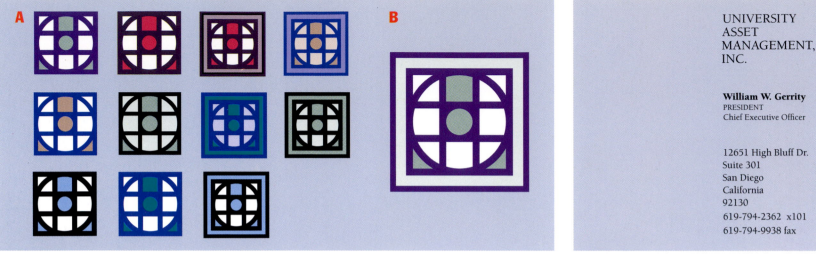

7 Choosing the color scheme

With the square mark chosen, the next step was to choose colors. Jill Davis developed several color schemes using custom (Pantone) colors (A). Bright colors were eliminated because the client felt they made the symbol look too much like stained glass. A bordered form of the design in blue and green was selected (B).

8 Adding type

To add lettering, Jill Davis chose Adobe's Berkeley font, both for its look and because it had 4 weights: Book, Medium, Bold, and Heavy. In general, she finds heavier-weight typefaces useful for names on business cards. To develop the lettering, she used Medium weight for the company name and Book weight (which was slightly lighter than Medium) for the address and phone number.

9 Developing the final logo

Jill Davis developed a final business card design (A), a letterhead application (B), and an envelope design (C), applying the blue and green colors of the logo mark to the type. To present these designs to the client in final form, she ordered internegative transfers (INTs) in the Pantone colors, and applied them with a burnishing tool to samples of paper and card stock. This allowed the client to see the true colors of the inks and paper, as well as see the paper texture.

26

Working with Type

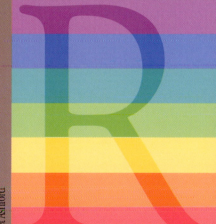

Janet Ashford

Though primarily a drawing program, Illustrator includes many sophisticated type functions that make it possible to create custom type treatments for headlines and logos.

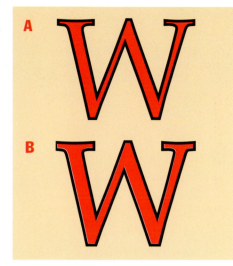

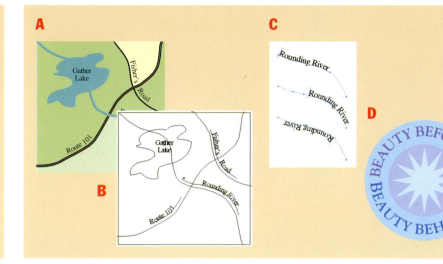

Stroking without "thinning"

Stroking a character can thin it because half the stroke width extends inside (A). To avoid this, apply a stroke of None, copy the letter, paste the copy in back, and stroke the copy at twice the stroke weight you want. Half the copy's stroke will extend beyond the edges of the original (B).

Using type along a path

Type along a path is often used on maps so that names of rivers and highways can follow the curves of these features (A). For this map we set curved type on paths drawn parallel to the paths we wanted to label (B). To move type on a path after it has been set, simply select it and drag the I-beam to the position you want. To flip type across the path, double-click on the I-beam (C). Type can be set around a circle by setting the top and bottom lines on 2 separate circles and then overlapping them (D). For a description of this technique see Chapter 19, "Creating a Braided Medallion" on page 56.

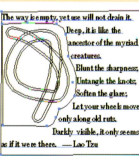

Wrapping type around an object

Type can be wrapped around a graphic object of any shape by combining the type and the graphic using the Make Wrap command. To control the way the type wraps (for example, to determine its distance from the graphic) it is useful to combine the type with a separate shape drawn around the graphic. We drew a graphic of a knotted rope and placed a paragraph of type over it (A). We then drew a shape around the graphic, selected both the shape and the type, and chose Make Wrap from the Type menu (B). Because the shape we combined with the type had no stroke or fill, it is not visible in the fin- ished graphic (C). The same technique can be used to wrap type around an initial capital letter (D).

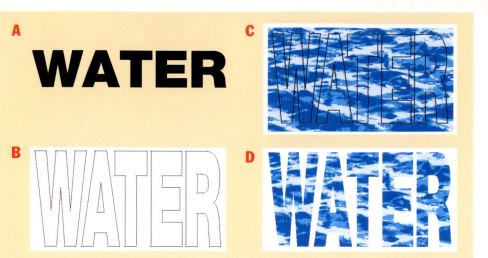

Filling type with gradations

Type outlines can be filled with gradients, which can then be manipulated with the gradient fill tool. We typed a word, chose Create Outlines to convert the letters to paths (A) and then used the Paint Style dialog box to fill the outlines with a gradient. This filled each letterform with the entire pink to blue gradient (B). We then selected the gradient tool and dragged it across the letters from top to bottom to change the direction of the gradient (C). Dragging the tool from left to right (D) and from center to right (E) spread the gradient through the letters as a group.

Using type outlines as a mask

To fill type outlines with a scanned image we first typed a word (A), converted it to outlines, moved the letters closer together, used the scale tool to change their height, and then converted the separate letterforms to a compound path by choosing Make from the Compound Paths submenu under the Object menu (B). We placed the letter outlines on top of a scanned water image, which was imported as an EPS file through the Place Art command (C). To mask the art into the outlines we selected both the outlines and the image and chose Make from the Masks submenu under the Object menu (D).

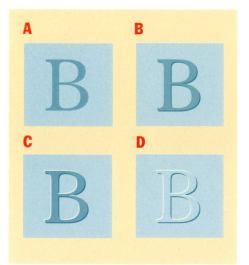

Creating shadowed or embossed type

To create a drop shadow we typed a letter (A), copied and pasted it behind, darkened its fill, and offset it down and right (B). To add a highlight, we lightened the fill of another copy and offset it up and left (C). To create an embossed look, we colored the top letter with the background fill (D).

Creating type effects with filters

The Pathfinder and Colors filters can be used to create special effects with type outlines. To create the look of intertwined letters we typed 2 letters, filled them with color, and converted them to outlines (A). We used the Pathfinder Outline filter to convert the letters into their component faces (B). An exploded view shows the letter's parts (C). We selected the piece where the center of the "S" overlaps the "L" and changed its fill to the darker color (D). To create various rainbow effects, we placed a white letter over a grid of colored bars (E) and applied the Soft filter at 100% to create a transparent look (F). We then selected the letterform shapes created by the filter and applied the Saturate More filter to darken them (G). We placed a green letter over the grid (H) and applied the Hard filter to simulate the look of overprinting (I). Finally, we deleted the letterform shapes and placed an inverted color grid behind the art (J).

27

Designing a Tourist Map

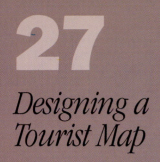

Illustrator was used to create the shapes, road lines, symbols and type for 2 maps of the California central coast, and to incorporate these elements into a 2-sided brochure with a cover panel and descriptive text.

YO

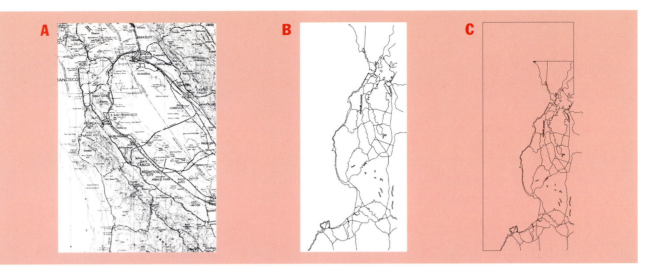

1 Starting with reference materials

Designers Maria Giudice and Lynne Stiles of YO in San Francisco worked with cartographer Scott Summers to create maps for a brochure for the Gray Line tour bus company. The designers used USGS (United States Geological Survey) maps as original references, like this one of the San Francisco Bay area (A). They traced the roads, coastline, northern direction, and scale by hand onto tissue paper, then scanned the tissue and saved it as a PICT for use as a template in Illustrator (B). They then traced over the template with the pen tool (C).

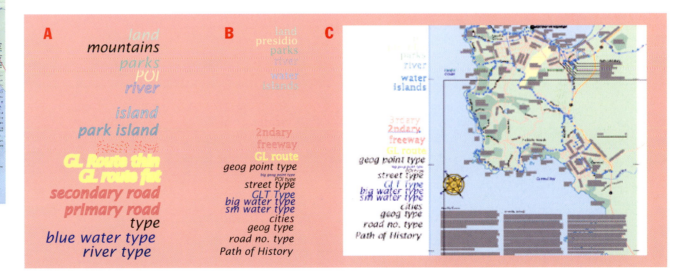

2 Grouping elements with names

The designers knew that the maps would contain many small elements and that they might want to experiment with colors and other attributes after the map was underway. To make selecting and editing easier, they typed a list of category names ("water," "island," "primary road," and so on) and positioned it on the Artboard at the side of each map. As each set of elements was created it was grouped with the appropriate name so that the group of objects could be selected simply by clicking on the name. Shown here are the lists for the central coast map (A) and the Monterey detail map (B), as well as a screen shot of the position of the Monterey list on the Artboard (C). ⚫ *A group of elements can also be isolated for easier selection by assigning it to a single layer using the Layers palette.*

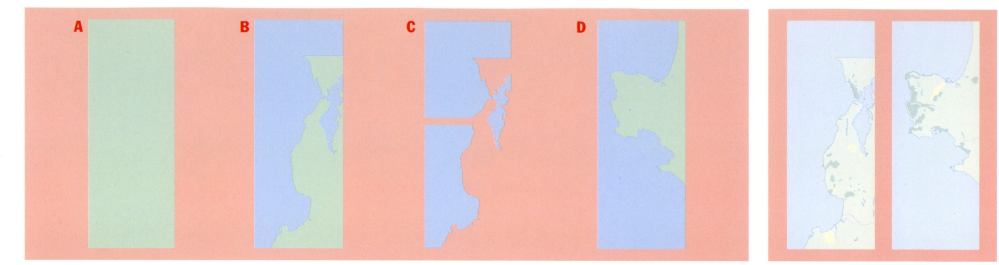

3 Building the background

The 2-sided brochure includes 2 maps showing the central coast area of California and a detail of Monterey. The maps were built up layer by layer starting with background shapes and moving upward to the type. Each map was created in a separate Illustrator file and began with a rectangle filled with light green to represent the land and drawn to the 9 x 23.5-inch finished size of the brochure (A). To define the central coastline, the designers created a large ocean shape with a light blue fill and 0.5-point dark blue stroke and positioned it over the land (B). Then, to avoid using a complex single path, they used the scissors tool to cut the ocean shape into 2 open paths, shown separated above (C). Because Illustrator automatically fills an open path, the 2 shapes are still filled with blue, but the stroke does not continue across the unclosed ends of the shapes. A single ocean shape was used to define the Monterey coast (D).

4 Defining parks and other features

To add further detail to the maps, the designers drew small shapes to indicate state parks and filled them with medium green. Shapes filled with yellow indicate points of interest. Lakes were created by drawing small shapes with the same stroke and fill as the ocean shapes.

5 Adding highways and roads

The designers created 4 line styles to distinguish different types of roads, including secondary roads (1-point stroke in a 60% tint of a custom color called "road") (A), primary roads (2-point stroke in 60% "road") (B), freeways (2-point stroke in 100% "road") (C), and the Gray Line Bus tour route (4.5-point stroke in 50% yellow) (D). To indicate the route taken by the bus, the designers copied the appropriate freeway and primary road lines, pasted them in front, and changed their stroke to the thick yellow line. The yellow lines were now positioned directly on top of the road lines. They used the scissors tool to cut the yellow lines into the segments they needed and deleted the unwanted segments. They selected all the remaining yellow lines, cut them to the clipboard, and then selected the grouped primary and freeway lines and chose Paste In Back from the Edit menu to paste the yellow route lines behind the road lines. A detail of the Monterey map shows the finished road lines in place (E). Road lines were drawn and positioned on both maps (F, G).

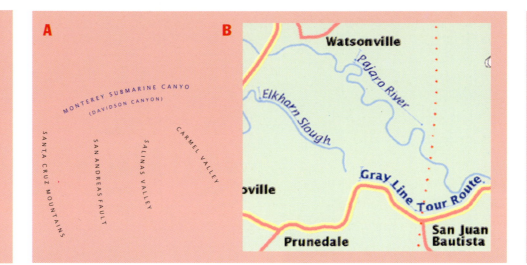

6 Defining type styles

To make the maps clear and easy to read, type for the place names was set in various sizes, styles, and colors of a single typeface, Lucida Sans, using regular, italic, and bold.

7 Using type on a path

Type for geographical features such as mountain ranges and valleys was set in Lucida Sans regular, in all caps, with a letterspace of 120%. (A few different letterspace values were used in particular circumstances.) The type was set along slightly curved paths drawn to follow the direction of the feature being designated (A). Type for rivers and route names was set in Lucida Sans Bold in blue, along curved lines drawn to follow the curves of the rivers or routes. In cases where the river was very curvy (as with the Pajaro River), the type was set on a less curved path so that it would be readable (B).

8 Creating highway signs

Numerals for highways were set in white, 6-point Univers Condensed Bold and placed over black symbols. A shield shape indicates an interstate highway while a circle indicates a state highway, following U.S. map convention. The shield shapes were drawn with the pen tool.

9 Drawing small symbols

The designers drew 7 small symbols to indicate places where pumpkins, garlic, artichokes, and flowers are grown and to designate the location of a whale migration route, an amusement park, and a lighthouse. The symbols were drawn by hand on tracing paper, scanned for use as templates, and then drawn over and refined in Illustrator. The symbols were designed to be simple, with solid color fills and thin black outlines so that they would be easy to recognize at a small size. The symbols are shown enlarged (A) and at actual map size (B).

10 Adapting pre-existing logos

The map brochure includes copies of the official logos of the Gray Line bus company (A), ASI (B), and the Monterey Bay Aquarium (C). The first 2 were drawn in Illustrator using scanned templates as guides. The aquarium logo was scanned from a stat, touched up in Adobe Photoshop, saved in EPS format, and imported into the Illustrator map file.

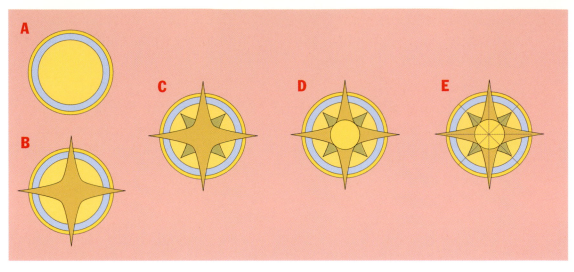

12 Constructing a compass rose

To create a compass rose, the designers first drew 3 concentric circles, each with a thin dark brown outline and a different color fill (A). A large pointed shape was created by using the pen tool to draw a single peak. It was copied and the copies were rotated in increments of 90 degrees and then joined (B). A smaller shape was created by copying the larger one, pasting it behind, rotating it 45 degrees, selecting its outer points, and dragging them into the inner circle using the scale tool (C). The designers added a small circle (D) and 4 gray lines, angled at 45-degree increments, which overlap the rose to create 8 spokes (E).

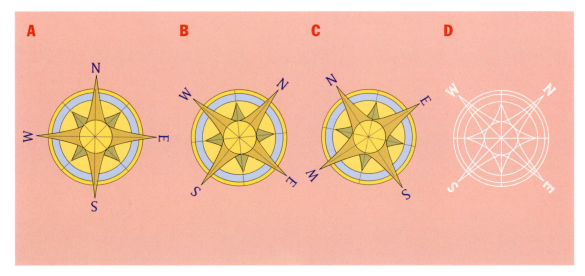

13 Rotating the compass rose

Initials that indicate the 4 directions were set in 10-point Lucida Regular in dark blue. The "N" for north was positioned at the top of the compass and the "E,", "S," and "W" for east, south, and west were rotated –90, 180, and 90 degrees respectively and positioned at the other 3 compass points (A). Copies of the finished rose were rotated about 45 degrees to fit the directions on the coastal map (B) and the Monterey map (C). In addition, a copy of the rose was styled with all the shapes and lines having a light gray stroke and no fill. This copy was used as a decorative element in the background of the brochure cover (D).

11 Positioning the type

The designers positioned the type and symbol elements in the appropriate map locations, being careful to space them in a pleasing way without overlapping them.

A

Montara

Gaspar de Portolá camped here during his 1769 expedition in search of Monterey Bay.

Gaspar de Portolá acampó aquí durante su expedición en busca de la Bahía de Monterrey en 1769.

Gaspar de Portolá zeltete hier im Jahre 1769 während seiner Expedition auf der Suche nach der Bucht von Monterey.

Gaspar de Portola' si accampo' qui, nel 1769, nel corso della sua spedizione in cerca della baia di Monterey.

Gaspar de Portola campa ici durant son expédition en 1769 à la recherche de la Baie de Monterey.

14 Importing an image as an EPS

To provide an image for a cover panel for the map brochure, the designers obtained a transparency of a sea otter from the Monterey Bay Aquarium, scanned it, and used Adobe Photoshop to delete the background and replace it with a solid background of 25% cyan. The image was saved at 300 dpi in CMYK EPS format and imported into Illustrator. The EPS's PICT preview would let the designers see the image on-screen. The photo image was positioned over the top panel of the brochure along with dark blue rules and the light gray version of the compass wheel, as shown in this screen shot.

B

Carmel-by-the-Sea and Mission Carmel

Formerly an artists' colony; Father Junipero Serra founded a mission here in 1771.

En el pasado fué una colonia de artistas. El Padre Junípero Serra fundó una misión aquí en 1771.

Früher eine Künstlerkolonie; Vater Junipero Serra gründete hier eine Mission im Jahre 1771.

In un recente passato una comunita' artistica; fu' dove nel 1771 Padre Junipero Serra fondo' una missione.

Autrefois une colonie d'artistes, le Père Junipero Serra y fonda une mission en 1771.

15 Finishing the cover panel

Once the graphic elements were in place, the designers added black type to complete the cover panel. The title of the tour map was set in 32/36-point Lucida Regular with an 80% horizontal scale applied to condense the letters and a track of −50/1000 em to kern them more tightly. The word "Welcome" was set in 5 languages in 21-point Lucida Sans Italic, also with an 80% horizontal scale. A box was drawn as a placeholder for the Japanese and Korean translations of "Welcome" which were typeset separately and stripped in later.

16 Setting brochure type

Both sides of the brochure include text describing points of interest. The type for the front (coastal map) is set in thin 1.375-inch columns with the subheads in 9/9-point Lucida Sans Bold and the text in 8/9-point Lucida Sans Regular (A). The type for the back is set in 2.625-inch columns with the leading increased to 11 for the subheads and 10 for the text to make the wider columns more readable. A track of −10/1000 em was applied to make the type fit the available space (B).

28

Layering Blends

Steve McGuire

Although Adobe Illustrator now provides gradient fills, blends still can't be surpassed for certain kinds of modelling of light and shadow. Steve McGuire used several kinds of blended effects, layered on top of each other, to model this alligator.

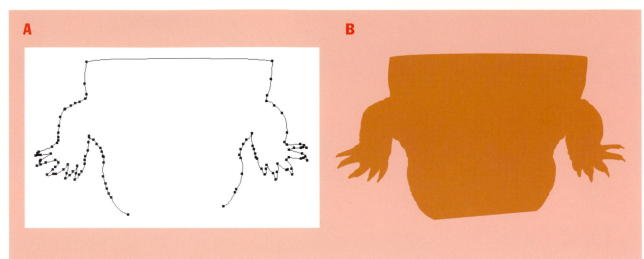

A   **B**

1 Defining the body shape
Steve McGuire began the alligator illustration by drawing an open-ended curve that defined the body of the 'gator (A) and specifying a solid fill color (B). He planned to use the filled object as a masking object that would trim the dark-to-light blends he would add later to round the form of the animal.

2 Defining the head and back
On top of the basic body shape McGuire drew another shape to contain the head and the ridge on the animal's back. This shape would also be used as a mask.

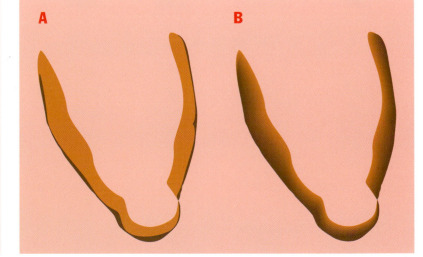

A   **B**

3 Blending between colored shapes
To define the rounded edges of the jaw, McGuire started with 2 pairs of shapes, 1 pair for each side of the jaw. A broad light shape and a narrower dark shape on top of its outside edge defined the left jaw, and a similar pair defined the right jaw (A). Blending the 2 pieces of each pair resulted in rounded jaws that looked light on top and shaded underneath (B).

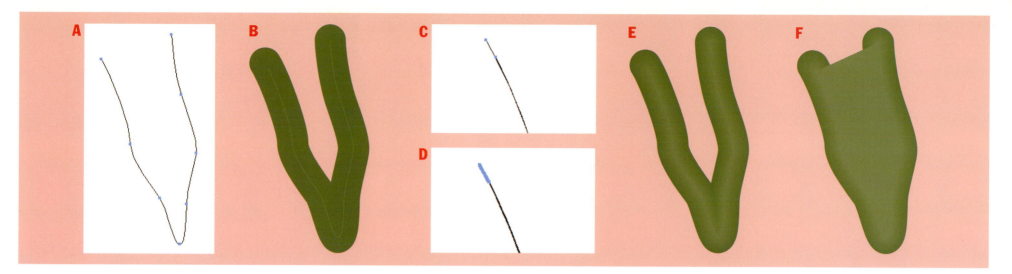

4 Blending layered lines

McGuire used a second kind of blend — between a thin light-colored round-ended stroked path and a thick dark round-ended stroked line beneath it — to color the snout. He began by drawing a V-shaped path (A), gave it a thick dark stroke, pasted a copy in front, and gave the copy a thin light stroke (B).

To make it easier to select the end points of the 2 lines for blending, he shortened the top line slightly so that the left end points of the 2 lines were separated and could be individually clicked with the blend tool (C). Blending resulted in a stack of lines (D) with a "neon" look (E). Assigning a fill to the top line filled in the space between lines (F).

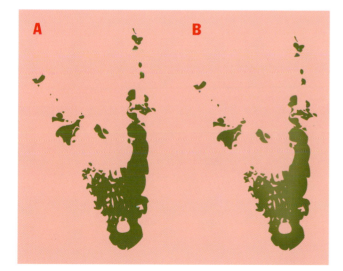

5 Masking the blend

A series of shapes were drawn and filled with green to define the mottled pattern on the top of the snout (A). The shapes were selected, converted to a compound path, and used to mask the blend made in step 4 (B).

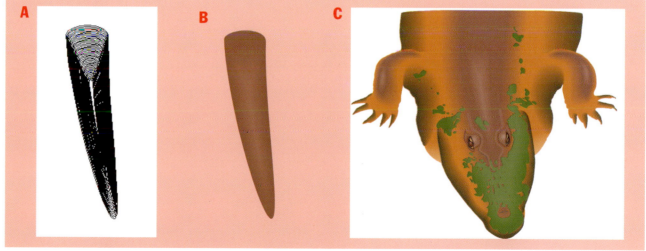

6 Modelling the limbs and the back ridge

The legs and the ridge on the back of the alligator were made by blending a larger dark filled shape with a smaller light shape on top (A, B). Masking the 3 kinds of blends — outside shading blends, line blends, and raised features — inside the 'gator outlines completed the basic artwork for the animal (C).

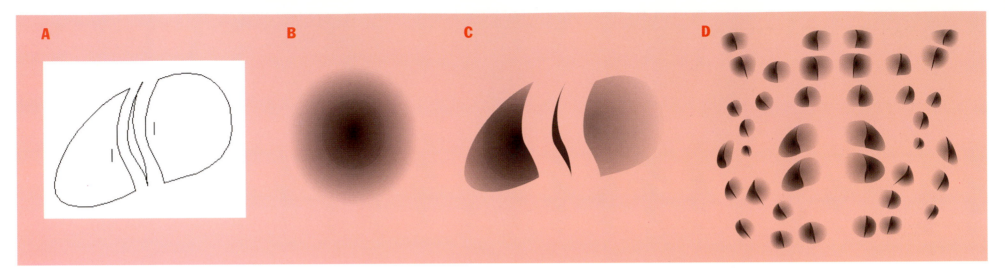

7 Adding secondary shading

McGuire was able to add complexity to the modelling of the 'gator by layering more blends on top. These dark-to-light blends, from a line of a high-percentage tint of black to a line of 0% tint of black, with both lines designated to overprint, built additional surface features by overprinting shading on top of the color blends he had already used. Each bump on the alligator's back was formed in 3 pieces (A). Each of the 2 large pieces was used to mask a blend between a short, round-ended, thin dark line and a short, round-ended, thick light line. Although shapes such as these bumps could be filled with radial gradients, using blends of lines instead introduces a slight deviation from perfect radial symmetry (B). A different blend was masked inside each of the 2 sides of the bump (C). McGuire drew several different bumps, selected and duplicated them, and flipped the duplicates across a vertical axis in the center of the alligator's back. He then moved or rotated some of the bumps, again avoiding perfect symmetry (D).

8 Completing the modelling detail

McGuire used similar dark-to-light overprinted blends to add shading to further round the body parts of the 'gator (A). He also drew black overprinted lines to define the animal's scales (B). Viewed on-screen, the dark-to-light blends were opaque and made the animal look "frosted" and unrealistic (C). But when output, the overprinted features became transparent (see opening illustration). ♣ *To be able to see overprinting on-screen, you can use the Hard filter.*

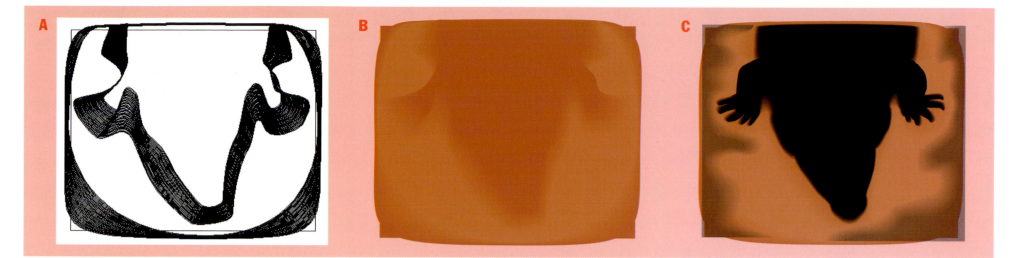

9 Shading the background

To shade the background, McGuire began by blending shapes in light and darker shades of tan. He started with the outline of the 'gator and an enlarged, widened version of the same shape; to control lighting at the edges of the background, he blended between rectangles with rounded corners, the inner shape more rounded than the outer (A, B). He then added the shadow under the 'gator's body as an overprinted dark-to-light blend and added much lighter overprinted shading as an irregular border for the background, to interact with the tan color gradient already in place (C).

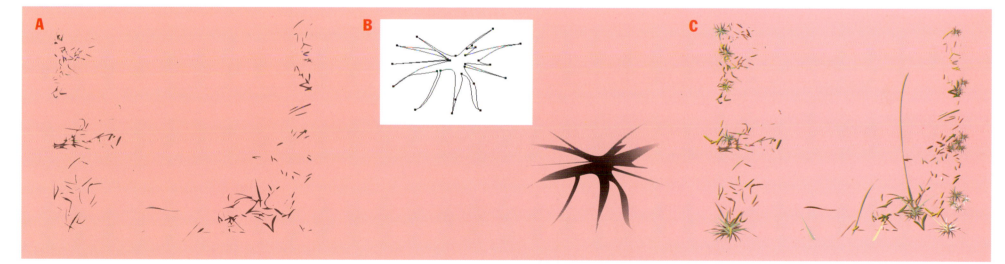

10 Adding background detail

McGuire drew plant shapes to fill the space around the 'gator. He duplicated the shapes, filled the set underneath with overprinted gray (A), and filled the top set with masked blends of greens (B). The bottom set was offset slightly, producing the effect of shadows under the plants (C). For the pebbly texture of the ground and other surfaces within the image, McGuire designed and applied pattern fills. But patterns add complexity to Illustrator files, and when he tried to output the file, the patterns made the output difficult. To simplify the output process, he used Adobe Photoshop to render the illustration by opening the Illustrator EPS file in Photoshop at a resolution of 300 dpi and saving the file in TIFF format; this new file could be output relatively easily.

29

Creating Electronic "Woodcuts"

Lin Wilson

Unlike traditional woodcuts, Lin Wilson's electronic versions are layered rather than carved. Wilson starts with a solid black shape and then layers the detailed shapes on top of it. The simple path structure makes the illustrations relatively easy to construct and quick to print and keeps the file sizes small so they can be quickly transferred to clients by modem.

1 Creating a background shape

For the spot illustration shown at the left, Lin Wilson began with a solid black-filled object that defined the overall shape of the portrait. The illustration would be printed on a white background, so rather than create the collar as a separate object, he broke the right edge of the black object with 3 points that define the collar as negative space.

2 Adding color

Wilson drew the small facial features and the curls that define the hair as no-stroke shapes filled with process colors and positioned them on top of the black background shape.

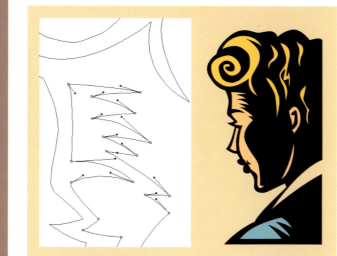

3 Creating a "carved" look

To create shading to show the curve of the face from light to shadow and the lighting on the curve of the shoulder, Wilson used shapes drawn with a series of corner points in a zigzag configuration to create an effect similar to the carving used in traditional woodcut technique.

4 Adding small details

The earring in the illustration consists of a round pink shape with black and white details. Rather than draw a complex pink shape that allowed black to show through, Wilson drew the earring with the circle tool (A) and added simple black and white shapes on top of it (B, C).

5 Increasing complexity

In another spot illustration Wilson again began with a solid black shape (A). This time he layered a white shape on top of it to create the negative space in the bottle's handle (B). He added shapes with zigzag edges to define light and shadow (C). He wanted all the lettering on the bottle's label to be outlined in black, so he drew a larger black "W" behind the red letter (D). Additional label detail and a shape behind the black layer to make the bottle's shadow completed the artwork (E).

6 Using a second background color

For an editorial illustration for a magazine article about changes in modern family life, Wilson created a series of 8 portraits in his woodcut style. Each portrait was carved out of black, as in the previously described artwork, but each also included a color background within the black frame. The bottom layer of each portrait is a 4-sided solid (A). The color block on top of it serves as background and also outlines the portrait (B). A layer of color-filled objects defines the major features of the portrait (C), and details such as facial features, the woman's beads, and the blue checks of the man's shirt are smaller objects (D). A large gray shape unifies the portraits and provides space for adding type later (E).

30

Creating an Airbrushed Look

Daniel Pelavin

For a striking image of 1930s Los Angeles, Daniel Pelavin used carefully crafted blends and gradient fills to produce the look of a traditional airbrushed illustration.

1 Creating a rough sketch

To begin an illustration of historical Los Angeles, New York illustrator Daniel Pelavin made a tight pencil sketch (A), scanned the sketch at 72 dpi, and opened it as a template in Illustrator, where it appeared as a gray image (B).

2 Creating custom colors

Pelavin knew that he would execute the illustration in a monochrome palette of gold tones. So before beginning the drawing he opened the Custom Color dialog box, clicked on the Process Color icon, and entered CMYK values to create a series of 6 custom colors ranging from bright to very dark gold. These appeared in the list along with previously created custom colors.

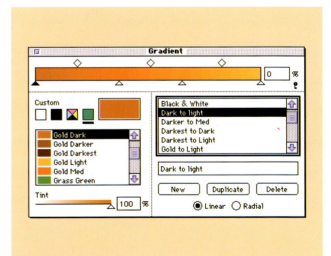

3 Defining gradients

Pelavin also knew that he would be making extensive use of gradient fills, so he used the Gradient dialog box to define and name a number of linear and radial gradient fills between various pairs of light and dark gold tones.

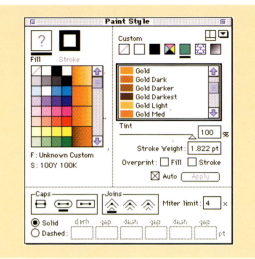

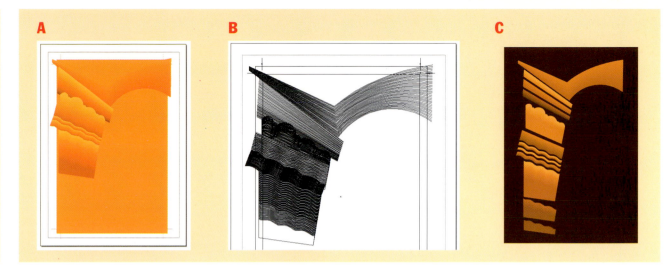

4 Preparing the color palette

The custom colors Pelavin had created now appeared in the Paint Style dialog box when the green custom color icon was selected. In addition, Pelavin clicked on the gradients icon and dragged his gradient color chips from the list into the larger squares in the Paint Style palette reserved for gradient fills, in order to have them easily available.

5 Constructing a sky background

The poster image is built up of several layers, beginning with a sky background. (The description that follows traces the creation of the elements of each layer, working from back to front, and then shows how the whole illustration comes together layer by layer.) To create the sky background, Pelavin drew a medium gold rectangle and layered over it number of curved and di-agonally slanted shapes to define clouds and areas of tonal shift in the sky (A). These were modeled to look 3-dimensional by using blends, both between pairs of straight lines and between pairs of curved lines. A view in Artwork mode shows the dense lines of the intermediate steps of the blends (B). To show the sky's components more clearly here, we changed the background to dark gold and moved the separate blended elements apart (C).

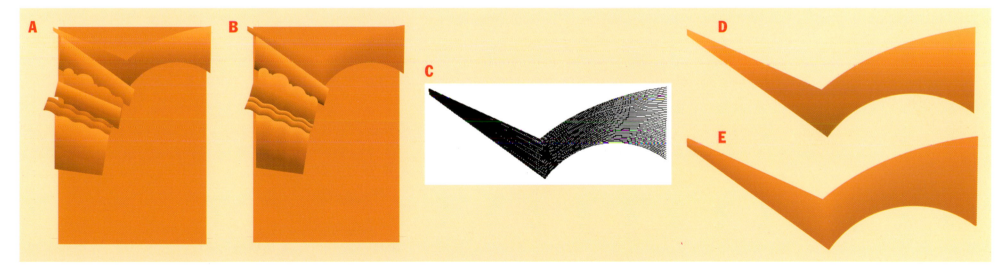

6 Using blends rather than gradients

Creating blends for each of the sky/cloud elements took time, but it was essential for producing the carefully crafted airbrushed look Pelavin wanted. If he had filled each of the shapes with a simple linear gradient, as shown here (A), the modeling would not have been as effective or followed the form of the shapes as closely as the blends do (B). A close-up of a blended shape in Artwork mode shows its construction (C). Close-ups of the same shape filled with a gradient (D) and the blended shape (E) show how the modeling produced by the blend is more effective.

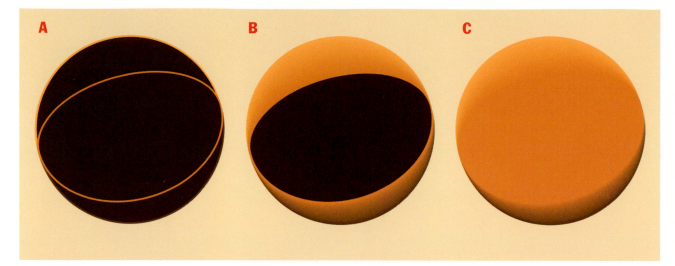

7 Modeling a circle with blends

The next layer in front of the sky background features a design of concentric circles representing waves from a broadcasting tower. To create the first modeled circle Pelavin drew a medium gold circle (shown here in dark gold for contrast) and positioned arcs cut from other circles to use as the starting and ending lines for 2 blends (A). The top blend creates a highlight by blending from light gold down to the medium gold of the background circle. The bottom blend creates a shadow by blending from dark gold up to the medium gold of the background (B). Because the inner lines are set to the same color as the background, the blends appear to fade into it. The effect is that of a slightly rounded disk with a light shining across it from the upper left (C).

8 Producing a pattern of concentric rings

Pelavin grouped his original circle with its blends, copied it, and chose Paste In Front to paste the copy in front of the original. Then he scaled the copy by clicking on its center and dragging with the scale tool until the new circle was reduced to about 70%. He repeated this process of copying, pasting in front, and scaling to produce the final pattern of 6 rings.

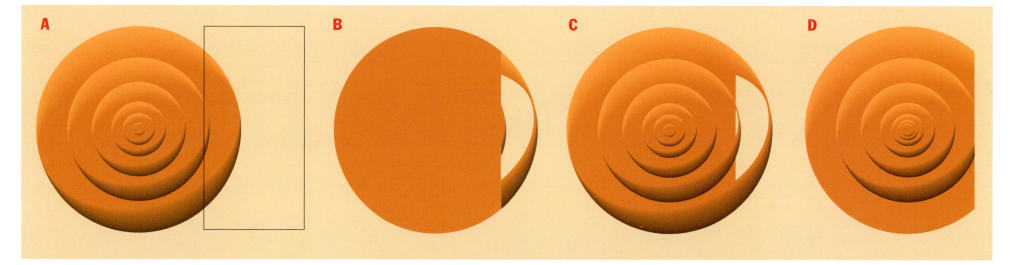

9 Using a Pathfinder filter to cut the rings

When the broadcast circles were positioned over the sky background they extended beyond the illustration. To eliminate the unwanted edges, Pelavin used the Minus Front filter to crop the 2 outer rings. To do this he drew a rectangle and positioned it in front of the rings (A). He then ungrouped the outer ring to separate it from its modeling blends. He selected the outer ring and the rectangle and chose the Minus Front command from the Pathfinder submenu under the Filter menu. This clipped off the right edge of the ring, which now lay in front of the ring pattern (B). Pelavin sent the clipped ring to the back and used the same technique to clip the next outer ring (C). To clip the blends he ungrouped them so he could delete the inner blended curves without deleting the original arcs used to create the blends. Then he used the scissors tool to trim back the original pairs of arcs, and finally he re-blended these arcs (D).

10 Blocking in building shapes

To create a dramatic rendering of the Los Angeles City Hall, Pelavin began by tracing over his template to produce 2 basic shapes that outline the tower and the base of the building. Both were filled with angled, linear gradient fills.

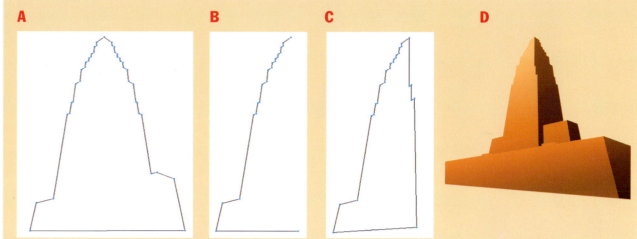

11 Creating highlight and shadow shapes

To make the building look 3-dimensional, Pelavin drew a large highlight shape for the front of the tower. To make the left edge of the highlight shape exactly match that of the background shape, he copied his original tower shape (shown here in Artwork mode) (A), cut the copy at the top center and bottom center and deleted the right-hand line segment (B), and then added a new path to join the 2 end points (C). He filled the highlight shape with a light-toned gradient that contrasts with the dark gradient in the background shape. He drew another small shape to create a highlight for a cube on the building, and drew a dark shadow shape for the building base (D).

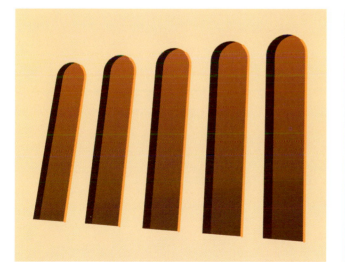

12 Blending multiple shapes to create details

To create archways for the bottom of the tower, Pelavin drew an arch shape and then copied and trimmed the copy to create a shadow shape and a highlight line. He copied, scaled, and sheared the arch to create a second arch and positioned it to the right. He then used the blend tool to create 3-step blends between each of the arches' 3 components to create the intermediate arches.

13 Finishing the city hall

Pelavin positioned the archways over the city hall shapes, drew additional angled window shapes that include highlight and shadow lines, and added more highlight and shadow shapes (as described in step 12) to model the rest of the building's architectural features.

14 Adding background building shapes

Pelavin used the same techniques of layering highlights and shadows over background shapes to create additional building elements and a street element. These were layered behind the completed city hall. All the buildings were rendered to look as though they were being lit by the same light source coming from the upper left.

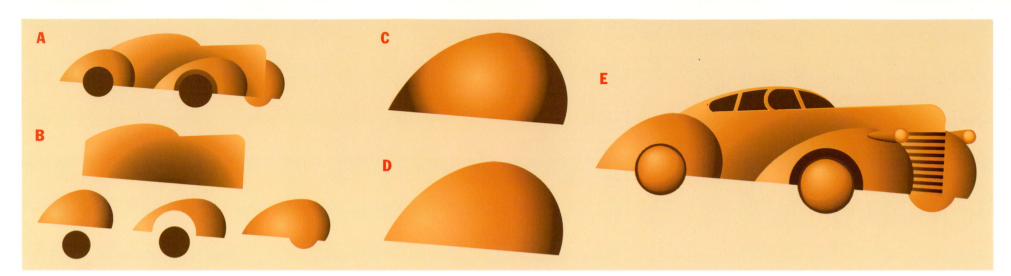

15 Constructing a car with radial gradients

To create a rounded, 1930s-style automobile, Pelavin began by drawing background shapes filled with radial gradients (A). An exploded view shows the body, fenders, and tire shapes that were layered to create the car (B). The radial fills were carefully modified to make the fender shapes look rounded. For example, Pelavin filled the rear fender shape with a radial gradient fill, which automatically appeared with the center of the fill at the center of the shape (C). He then used the gra-

dient fill tool to reposition the fill so that its center was near the left edge of the shape (D). Pelavin added window shapes, grilling, headlights, and other details to complete the car (E). ◆ *To modify a linear or radial gradient fill, click with the gradient fill tool pointer at the place where you want the gradient to begin, drag along the angle you want, and release the mouse at the point where you want the gradient to end.*

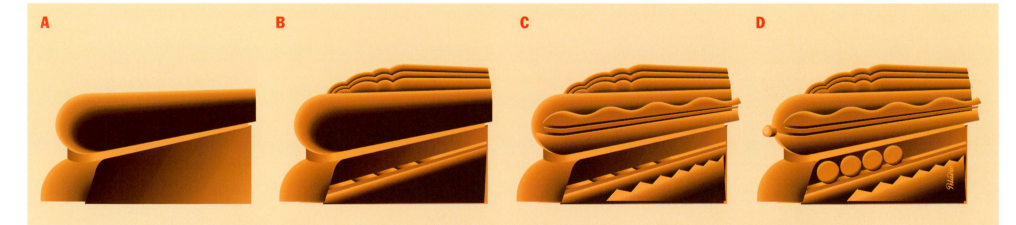

16 Constructing a train with shapes and blends

The streamlined train in the bottom right of the illustration was created by layering many blended shapes. Pelavin began by creating a bottom layer of 4 basic shapes, each filled with a blend or a gradient (A). He continued to add details to define the train, including steam constructed of wavy blends (B, C). The 4 wheels are scaled copies of the blended, 3-dimensional circle used for the broadcast tower (D).

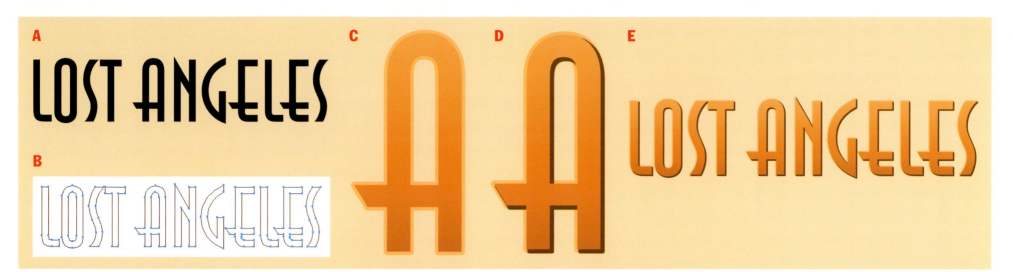

17 Creating custom type for the title

Pelavin began the illustration title by setting it in ITC Anna, a typeface which he had previously designed and licensed (A). He used the Create Outlines command to convert the type to outlines, shown here in Artwork mode (B). Then, to give the title the look of raised metallic letters, Pelavin filled each of the letterform shapes with a gradient from light gold down to medium dark gold. To create a highlight, he used Command-C, -B (Copy and Paste In Back) to paste a copy of each letter in back of its original. He gave the copies a fill of None and a heavy, light gold stroke, as shown here on the letter "A" (C). He then copied the originals again, pasted the copies in back, filled them with dark gold, and offset them slightly down and to the right to create a shadow (D). Because the Paste In Back command pastes an element in back of whatever elements are selected, the dark, shadow element was pasted in back of the original lettering but in front of the highlight copy. The finished type looks shiny and beveled, with the effect of light shining across it from top left to bottom right (E), corresponding to the lighting of the other parts of the illustration.

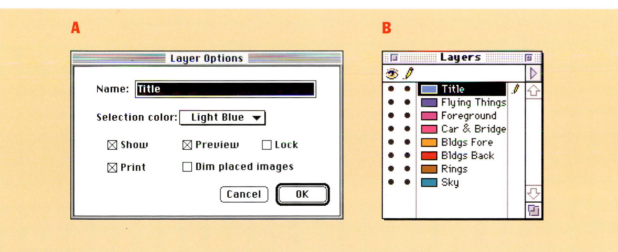

18 Using the Layers palette

The Layers palette is used to create separate layers in an illustration, so that you can isolate a layer and work on its elements without disturbing objects in other layers. Pelavin created 8 layers to manage his illustration. To create each layer he chose New Layer from the Layers palette pop-up menu and entered a name in the Layer Options dialog box. He chose a color to represent each layer and clicked on the additional options he wanted (A). The Layers palette shows the names and color codes, and provides 2 columns that make it possible to hide or display (under the eye icon) and lock or unlock each layer (under the pencil icon) (B). Layers are stacked in the order in which they are created, with the first-created layer at the top. But the layer order can be changed by simply dragging layer names to new positions in the palette.

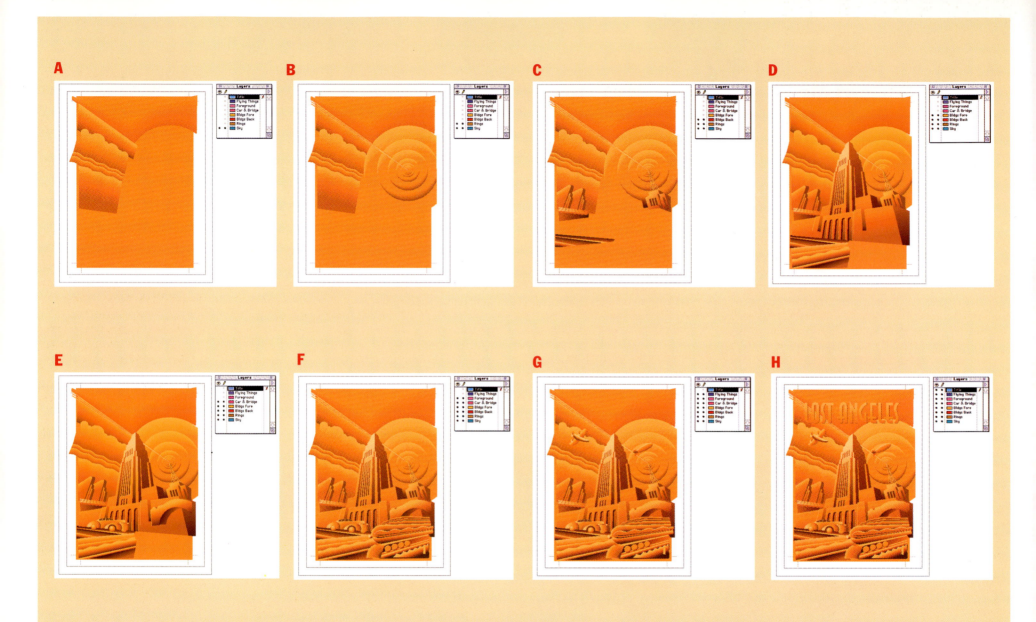

19 Building the illustration in layers

This sequence of screen captures shows how Pelavin's illustration was built up layer by layer. The first shot shows the lowest layer, named "Sky" in the Layers palette (A). The Layers palette to the right of the screen shot shows that only the Sky layer is currently visible. To show how the drawing was built, we made the layers visible one after another by clicking in the "eye" column of the Layers palette (B–H). Rather than spend time clipping or masking the edges of all the illustration elements, Pelavin drew crop marks to indicate the boundaries of the illustration. ● *To create crop marks, use the rectangle tool to draw a rectangle that defines the boundaries of the illustration. Then, with the rectangle selected, choose Cropmarks from the Object menu and choose Make from the submenu. Crop marks will automatically replace the rectangle and will print when the illustration is printed to paper or film. To eliminate crop marks, choose Cropmarks from the Object menu and choose Release from the submenu. The original rectangle will reappear and can be retained or deleted.*

31

Tying a Knot

Janet Ashford

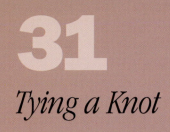

A careful use of filters makes it possible to create various visual illusions, including the look of a knotted rope that passes in front of and behind itself.

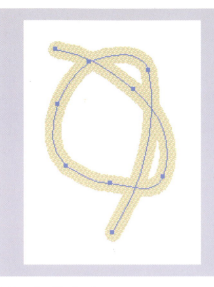

1 Drawing the knot

To begin the knot illustration used in Chapter 26, we used the freehand tool to draw a curved path, following the look of a knotted rope used as a visual reference. We assigned a thick beige stroke and round end caps.

2 Creating an edge

To create an edge in a contrasting color, so that our eyes could follow the course of the knot, we copied the original path, pasted the copy in back, and then increased the stroke width and applied a darker color.

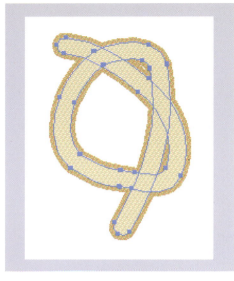

3 Using the Outline Stroke filter

We then converted the 2 rope elements from stroked paths to outlined shapes by selecting each one individually and applying the Objects, Outline Stroke filter from the Filter menu. The top shape is selected here.

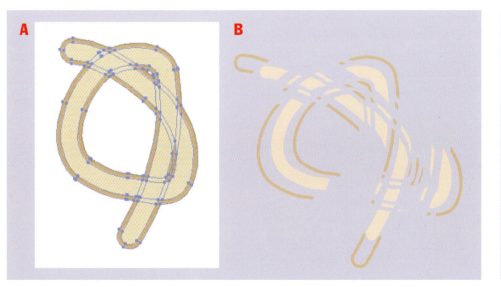

4 Using the Divide filter

We then selected both shapes and chose the Pathfinder, Divide filter from the Filter menu. This divided the shapes into small sections that defined every area in which the shapes overlapped (A). An exploded view shows the separate pieces created by the filter (B). Note: The results are different if the filter is applied to each shape one at a time.

5 Finishing the design

To create the visual illusion we wanted, we selected the appropriate small edge shapes and changed their fill color from beige to brown to make it look like the rope was tied in a knot.

32

Designing a Series of Book Covers

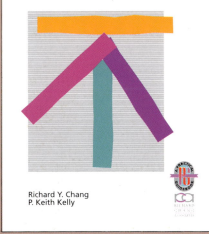

John Odam

Application of Illustrator 5.5's plug-in Distort filters at settings lower than the defaults can stylize a set of matching illustrations without giving them an obviously computer-generated look.

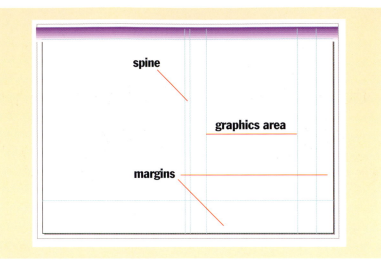

1 Creating the basic cover design

Designer John Odam wanted a businesslike but friendly and approachable look for a series of books on management topics. He began by using Illustrator's rulers to set guidelines to define the spine of the book and the area on the front cover where the graphics and type would be. At the top of the cover, extending across the front, spine, and back of the book, he created a rectangle and filled it with a gradient from purple to white.

2 Adding the series name

Working within this gradient rectangle, he added the name of the series in OPTICorvinus Skyline all caps. By inserting the type tool and repeatedly pressing Option–right arrow, he spaced the type across the entire width of the space reserved to hold the graphic. ❖ *Use Option-Shift–right arrow to open the spacing at 5 times the rate achieved with Option–right arrow.*

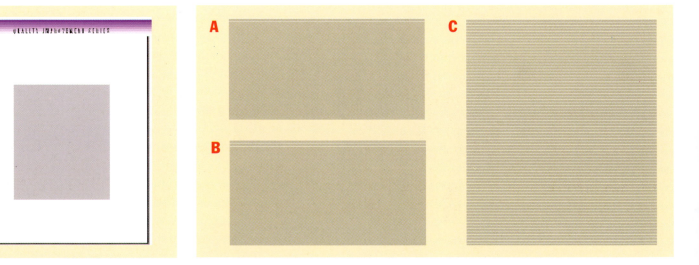

3 Adding a background for the graphics

In the center of the front cover Odam drew a gray-filled rectangle that would help to unify the series and would anchor the graphic for each book cover.

4 Adding pin stripes

The gray rectangle served as the basis for adding a pin-striped look to invoke the management theme of the book. Odam drew a white line with the pen tool and Shift key (A). He held down the Option key and dragged a copy of the line downward (B). He pressed Command-D (Repeat Transform) several times to repeat the duplication and move until the entire rectangle had been striped (C). ❖ *Repeat Transform works with the move, scale, shear, reflect, and rotate functions.*

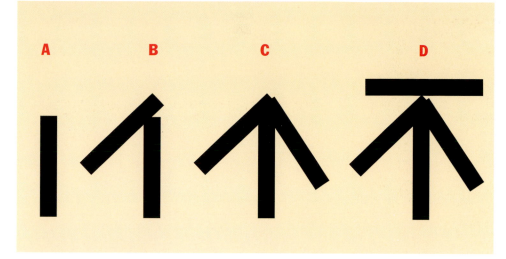

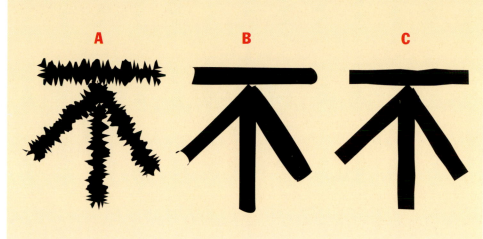

5 Designing simple graphics

After grouping the elements of the pinstripe background rectangle and locking them in place with the Lock command, Odam used the rectangle and oval tools to draw the simple shapes that would serve as the main cover illustrations. For the cover of *Improving Through Benchmarking* he started with a vertical rectangle (A), copied it, and used the rotate tool to move it into position as 1 arm of an arrowhead (B). He added another arm (C) and then a horizontal copy (D).

6 Roughening the shapes

To make the simple graphics less formal and more interesting, Odam experimented with 2 of the Distort filters, Roughen and Scribble. He found that the default settings for Roughen distorted the shapes far more than he wanted (A). The effect of Scribble was more subtle but tended to round the shapes and sometimes left "tails" at the corners (B). To get the effect he wanted, Odam reduced the Size and Detail settings of the Roughen filter to 1 or 2 (C).

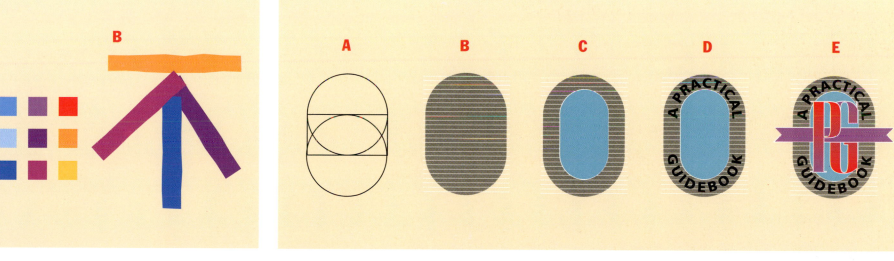

7 Coloring the illustration

Odam developed a palette of 12 colors to use for the graphics for the series of book covers (A). From these he chose 4 to apply to the parts of this illustration (B). Once he had colored parts of the illustration, he used the Bring To Front and Send to Back commands to arrange the parts.

8 Building a logo

To render the "Practical Guidebook" logo, he built the oval from 2 circles and a rectangle (A). To combine the 3 figures into a single object, he applied the Pathfinder Unite filter. He added pinstripes by the same method he had used for the background square (see step 4) (B). Because the background was white, the same color as the pinstripes, there was no need to mask the stripes inside the oval shape. He copied and reduced the oval, using the scale tool to scale it from the center, and filled it with a light blue (C). Then he set type on a path (D). He added the letters "P" and "G" (converted to objects with the Create Outlines command from the Type menu) with a white stroke and gradation fills, layering them with a banner (E).

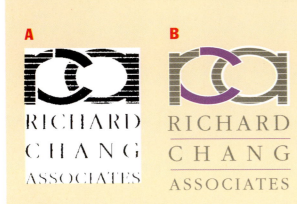

A **B**

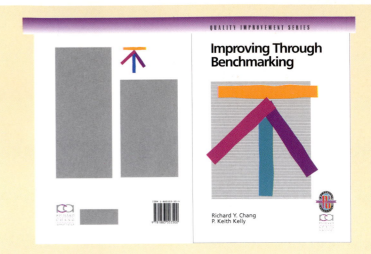

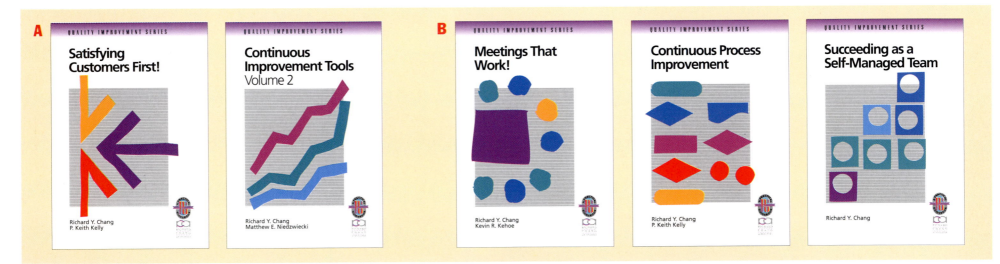

9 Tracing the publisher's logo

Odam scanned a printed version of the publisher's logo (A) and opened the scan as a template for a new file in Illustrator. He drew the 3 large letters by tracing with the pen tool, set the type with the type tool, and then converted it to outlines (B). He saved the file, selected all, and copied the logo to the clipboard so he could paste it onto the book cover.

10 Creating a bar code

Odam used BarCode Pro, a program that can generate a wide variety of codes — such as ISBN, SKU, and postal — to set the ISBN code for the back of the book. BarCode Pro can produce the codes as encapsulated PostScript files (as used here) or as PICT graphics.

11 Completing the cover

Odam set the title type in 44-point Frutiger bold and the authors' names in 18-point Frutiger, both flush left. He placed the "Practical Guidebook" logo in the lower right corner of the book cover along with the publisher's logo. For the back cover he repeated the main graphic, without the pinstripe background, and added the bar code, saving space for the blocks of text that would be supplied by the publisher.

12 Designing the other book covers

For the other books in the series, Odam designed similar covers, starting with the cover he had made. In each case he removed the main graphic and replaced it with new art. He used the Roughen filter for some (A) and the Scribble filter (with Horizontal and Vertical settings of 5) for others (B). The illustration for *Succeeding as a Self-Managed Team,* was created by layering circles over rectangles, applying the Scribble filter to the circles, and then selecting each circle and its rectangle and choosing Compound Paths from the Object menu so that the distorted circle became a hole in the rectangle. For the title and the authors' names, he selected the existing type with the type tool and entered the new information to replace the old. The new bar code for the back cover of each book was imported, positioned over the old bar code, and sent to the back; then the old code (now on top) was selected and deleted, leaving the new bar code in place.

33

Designing & Illustrating a Children's Book

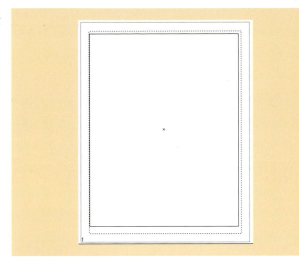

Lance Hidy

Illustrator's typesetting and page layout capabilities make it possible to create, size, and position illustrations for producing single pages or page spreads.

1 Defining the page

To design the pages for author Carolyn Coman's *Losing Things at Mr. Mudd's,* Lance Hidy began with Illustrator's default 8.5 x 11-inch page, drew a 7 x 9-inch rectangle with the rectangle tool to define the book page, and fixed it in place with the Lock command so it could not be nudged out of place accidentally.

2 Placing guides

Hidy created guidelines to indicate inside, outside, top, and bottom margins for both right and left pages. The tall rectangle defined by Hidy's guidelines indicated the maximum dimensions for an illustration, such as that shown in the title bar at the left, which filled a page without text and which was also used on the cover of the book. ⚫ *You can make guidelines by displaying the rulers and dragging guidelines from the rulers onto the page.*

Lucy climbed the stairs to her bedroom, closed the door, and flopped down on her bed. She was miserable. Not only had she lost her ring and her temper, but it just so happened that she was close to losing a tooth. She felt as if she was losing everything. "Oh brother," she said, and then let out a big, deep sigh.

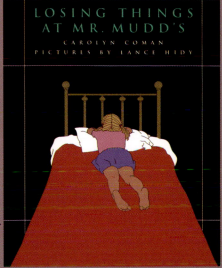

3 Specifying type

Hidy used Stone Informal for the book's text, set at 12 points on 18-point leading. The characters of this typeface are both very legible and interesting to look at. Varying stroke weights and carefully crafted details give the letters a well-grounded but lively look. Text was set flush left rather than justified so that letterspacing and word spacing were completely uniform. The bottom baseline of the text block was aligned with the bottom margin guide.

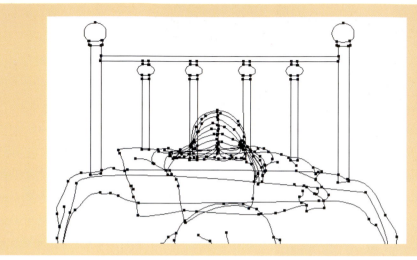

4 Making a template

Hidy began each illustration for the book by taking a 35mm photo of the scene he wanted to show, with models and props positioned as he wanted them to appear. Through a series of steps involving scanning, laser-printing the scanned image, drawing over the important lines in the scan, rescanning, and retouching in Adobe Photoshop, Hidy arrived at a line drawing he could open as a template and trace in Illustrator's artwork and template mode.

5 Tracing the line work

Hidy drew over the template with Illustrator's pen tool, placing points to define curves. He used few enough points so the curves would be smooth but placed them to give the line work a hand-drawn, not mechanical, quality. Hidy made his initial templates and line drawings larger than the finished illustrations would be, to give himself enough room to work.

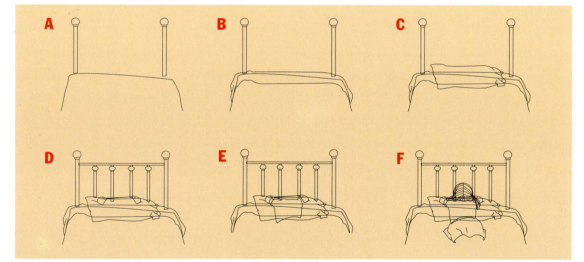

6 Overlapping shapes

Because the shapes he was outlining would be filled with solid colors, Hidy found it easier and more efficient to overlap them, building illustrations from back to front (A–F), layering clothing and hair shapes on top of arms, legs, and faces, for instance, rather than fitting the shapes together exactly.

7 Defining line style and weight

After making the line drawings, Hidy selected all the line work and assigned rounded end cap and join styles. Working at large but not necessarily uniform sizes, he waited until he had reduced the drawings to their final size before assigning a line weight of 0.7 or 0.8 point in the Paint Style palette. The line work is shown here close-up on the left and at final size on the right.

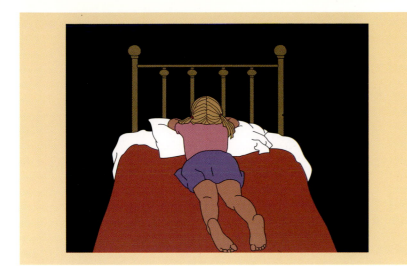

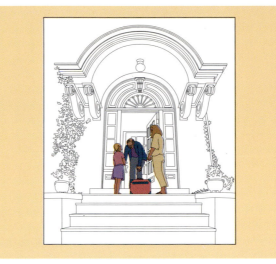

8 Coloring the shapes

Hidy filled each of his layered shapes with a flat color. The black lines were set to overprint the shapes they outlined. This provided *trapping*, a precaution that prevented unwanted white gaps from showing between areas of color when the book was printed. (For more about trapping, see "Trapping Artwork" on page 126.)

9 Varying the line weight

Hidy sometimes departed from his standard 0.7-point line weight and used a thinner line (0.5-point) in illustrations with quite a bit of background detail. To further simplify the detailed artwork and focus attention on the important part of the picture, Hidy omitted the color from some of the background shapes.

10 Omitting the line

For some shapes he omitted the line altogether. For example, although Lucy's thick hair was always defined by lines, Mr. Mudd's thinning hair was represented by gray shapes without outline.

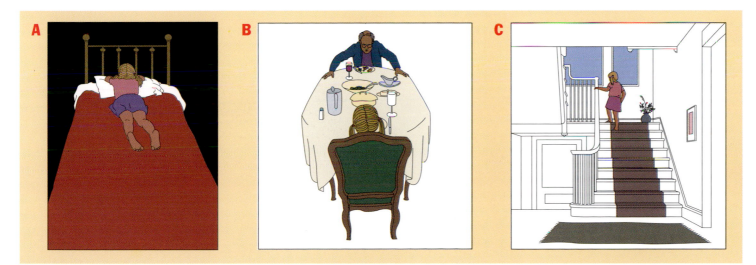

11 Directing the eye

Hidy's color selection set the mood in each illustration, and he used the contrast between dark and light colors to guide the eye to the subjective center of the picture (A) or to emphasize an interaction (B) or to show a direction of movement (C).

12 Standardizing color

Hidy defined his colors as Custom colors, with names that indicated what they were used for. This made it easy to keep the colors of hair and clothing constant throughout the book, except where he wanted a lighter or darker shade to indicate lighting conditions.

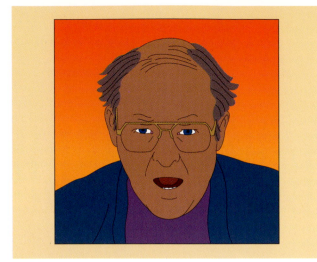

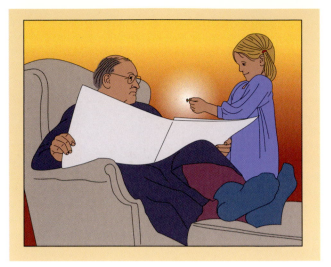

13 Using simple color gradients

In addition to the flat color used throughout the book, Hidy used simple gradations from 1 color to another for some backgrounds. He created the backgrounds in Illustrator or imported them as EPS files from Adobe Photoshop. Photoshop's Add Noise filter was applied to "soften" the color gradient and to reduce *banding,* an unwanted "striped" appearance.

14 Using multi-step gradients

In other cases, 3-color gradations were used. Hidy created these as abutting color blends in Photoshop. ● *In Illustrator 5.5, you can make multi-step color gradients by defining a starting and an ending color in the Gradient dialog box, then clicking below the gradient bar to add other color points and choosing a color to correspond to each new point.*

15 Using radial gradients

Radial gradients were combined with linear gradients by masking in Photoshop, and these were imported into the back layer of some of the Illustrator drawings to focus attention on small but important objects, such as the ring in this picture. Hidy used the rulers in Illustrator and Photoshop to pinpoint the center of the radial gradients, such as the position of the ring.

16 Using photomontage and blended shapes

Hidy used photomontage in some illustrations and created blends from 1 shape to another to add dimension to subjects such as the goldfish and the pink globe in the picture above. A photomontage, imported as an EPS file from Photoshop, was used for the picture of the cat. A blend from a larger pink outer shape to a smaller white inner shape was used to form the glow on the pink globe on the shelf. The pectoral fins of the fish at the right were formed by masking blended lines inside the fin shapes. (Notice also that the stripe pattern on the wallpaper is another instance of using color without outlines, which serves to flatten or thin the colored object.)

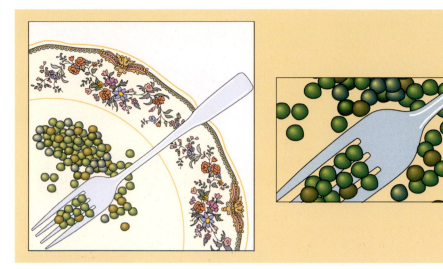

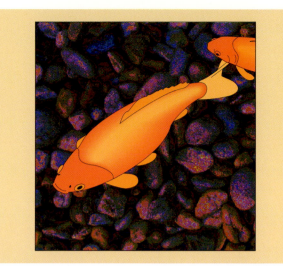

17 Scanning a 3D object

The plate for a dinner illustration was drawn from a scan made by putting a china plate upside directly on the bed of a desktop scanner. Once Hidy had traced 1 instance of the flower pattern from the scanned plate, he copied it and rotated the copy into position using the rotation tool. (Hidy created all the peas by repeating only 7 different blended shapes. The highlight on the fork and the gold lines on the plate are further examples of color without the black outline.)

18 Making backgrounds from photos

Scanned photos, which Hidy altered in Photoshop by "scrambling" the colors, were incorporated into some pictures, such as the illustration of the goldfish in the backyard pond. (By resizing with Illustrator's scale tool, Hidy was able to use the same goldfish for the pond and for the picture on the wall, shown previously.)

19 Assembling the pages

Hidy adjusted some illustrations by cropping or resizing so they would fit with the text on their pages. He placed a 1-point black border around each picture.

20 Making printer spreads

Pages were assembled into files that included 2 pages each, paired as the printer would need them for folding and binding the pages for the 32-page book. (To end the book, shown here, Hidy used center alignment for the type and shaped it into a triangle by pressing the Return key after the words he wanted to include in each line. He used a character from the Caslon Ornaments font as an end symbol.)

34

Designing an Invitation

Jim Walcott-Ayers and Liz Pollina

Designers from Walcott-Ayers Group used simple illustrations and type generated in Illustrator to compose an eye-catching 2-color invitation.

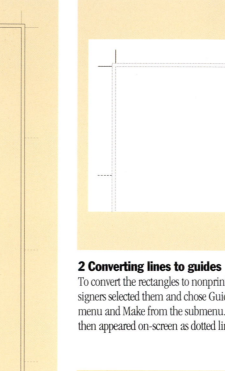

1 Drawing guidelines and cropmarks

Designers Jim Walcott-Ayers and Liz Pollina used the Document Setup dialog box to open a Custom 18 x 18-inch artboard and drew a 16 x 5.5-inch vertical rectangle to mark the boundaries of the paper they planned to use. They copied the rectangle, pasted the copy in front, and chose Cropmarks from the Object menu and Make from the submenu to replace the rectangle with cropmarks at its four corners. They then drew a second rectangle to mark the boundaries of a 0.125-inch bleed outside the crop marks and additional short lines specified with dashed lines to mark where the invitation would be folded down to 4 panels of 4 x 5.5 inches each to fit a standard-size invitation envelope.

2 Converting lines to guides

To convert the rectangles to nonprinting guides, the designers selected them and chose Guides from the Object menu and Make from the submenu. The rectangles then appeared on-screen as dotted lines.

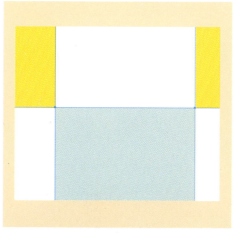

3 Using Snap To Point

Working on screen, without rough sketches, the designers drew a series of color-filled rectangles and placed them inside the guides. To make sure that the corners of the rectangles aligned exactly, they turned on the Snap To Point option in the General Preferences dialog box from the Edit menu. The corner points of the rectangles in the detail above are exactly on top of each other.

4 Creating a pattern

The designers continued to draw and position turquoise and yellow rectangles until they had filled the design area with the elements they needed to serve as backgrounds for the drawings and type they intended to add.

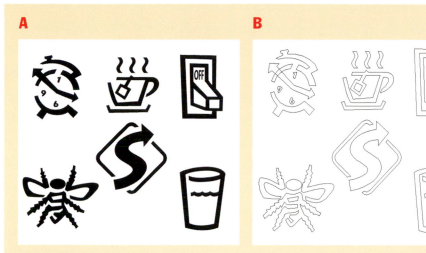

A

B

A

B

C

D

5 Creating illustrations

The invitation is for a golf tournament called the BS Cup, sponsored by 2 wineries in the Napa Valley of California, Bouchaine Vineyards and Saintsbury. Proceeds are donated to local charities and organizations, including the Napa Valley Opera House. The event and the invitation are meant to be light-hearted, so the designers came up with the idea of using rebuses (picture puzzles in which simple icons or numerals stand in for words to create a message) (A). The icons were drawn directly in Illustrator and are constructed of simple closed shapes rather than lines (B).

6 Converting type to outlines

To create numerals for one of the picture puzzles, the designers used the type tool to set them in 32-point Lithos Bold (A) (shown larger above) and chose the Create Outlines command from the Type menu to convert the characters to font outlines (B). They used the scale tool to apply a vertical scale of 120% (C), filled the outlines with yellow, and then staggered the numerals by moving the second and fourth ones down slightly (D).

A

B

7 Arranging the icons

The icons were positioned in rows on the top 2 panels of the invitation and filled with white, turquoise, or yellow to contrast with the backgrounds. Below each icon is a letter in parentheses set in 8-point Lithos Bold and keyed to an answer code in the corner of each panel.

8 Creating a version for comping

The designers planned to print the invitations in 2 opaque colors on a textured gray paper. To get a corresponding view on-screen and in color proofs printed during the design process, they temporarily filled the white elements with 25% gray.

9 Setting type on a corner angle

The answer to each picture puzzle appears in the corner of each panel set in 8-point Lithos Regular in all caps with a horizontal scale of 81%. To make the type go around the corner on the top panel, the designers used the pen tool to draw a 90-degree corner, selected the path-type tool, positioned the cursor toward the bottom of the vertical line of the angle, and typed the text, which automatically flowed around the corner (A). They then rotated the type 180 degrees (B). ✦ *Lines drawn for placing type along a path are visible in Artwork mode but not in Preview mode and do not print.*

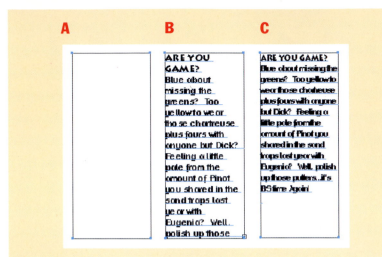

10 Setting type in a rectangle

To set body type within the columns in the bottom 2 panels of the invitation, the designers selected the type tool and dragged with the cursor to create a rectangle that fit a single column width (A). Then they entered text and specified 10-point Lithos Black for the subheads and 10-point Insignia A for the body type (B). Not all the type fit into the rectangle, so the designers applied a Horizontal Scale of 81% to all the type to condense it (C).

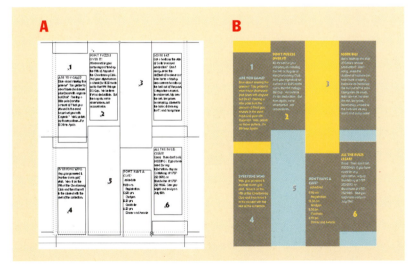

11 Positioning type and numerals

The designers set 6 units of rectangle type and positioned them in the columns of the lower 2 panels. They then set numerals in 22-point Lithos Black with an 81% Horizontal Scale to help lead the reader's eye from block to block. The elements are shown above in Artwork mode (A). They then specified color for the type, alternating between turquoise and yellow (B).

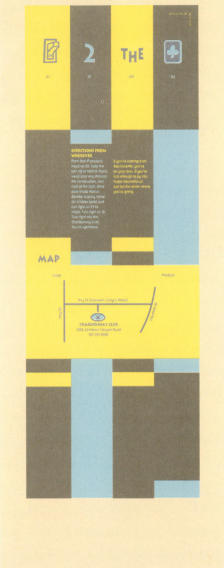

12 Designing the back of the invitation

The back of the invitation includes another picture puzzle, directions, and a simple map drawn with the pen tool. The designers used the same illustration style, type specifications, geometric elements, and colors as for the front.

13 Designing a reply card

A matching 4 x 5.5-inch reply card was mailed with each invitation. The front of each card features a picture puzzle using the same kind of illustrations and type used on the invitation. It is shown above both in the 2-color version used for output (A) and the 3-color version used for screen viewing and color proofing (B).

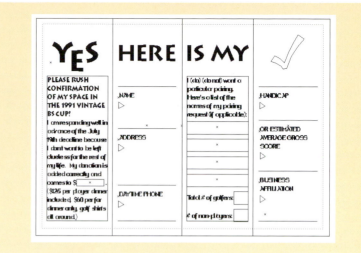

14 Setting headline type for the reply card

The headline for the back of the reply card was set in 3 different colors and spreads across the first 3 columns of the card, but is actually a single line of type. The designers first set the type in 42- and 32-point Lithos Bold (A) and then applied a Baseline Shift of −12 points to the "E" in "YES" to lower it and a Baseline Shift of +3 points to the next 3 words to raise them (B). To kern the "Y" and "E" so that they were closer together, the designers selected the 2 letters and pressed Option–left arrow to pull the "E" to the left. The type to the right of the "E" also moved to the left (C).

15 Positioning elements on the reply card

The designers set type in rectangles for the body text of the reply card back and assembled these with point type (type set in lines) and with rectangles drawn to contain information supplied by the event participants.

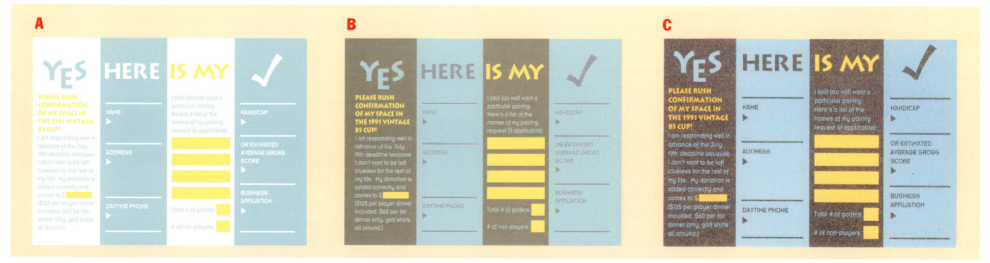

16 Finishing the reply card

The designers created a 2-color version of the reply card back by assigning turquoise and yellow to those elements they wanted to print in those inks, and assigning white to those elements that should knock out (A). They also created a 3-color version with gray replacing white for screen viewing and comping (B). The 2-color files for both invitation and reply card were output as spot separations and printed as opaque inks on a textured gray paper. But the ink coverage was not good enough, so the printer stripped in a gray mezzotint texture and printed the pieces on white paper (C).

35

Creating a Poster

Jim Walcott-Ayers and Meghan Kelley

To create a colorful tabloid-sized poster on recycling, designers from Walcott-Ayers Group used Pantone colors and Illustrator's simple drawing tools combined with some powerful filters for editing shapes.

1 Drawing rough sketches

Designers Jim Walcott-Ayers and Meghan Kelley were asked to create a poster for the annual conference of the California Resource Recovery Association. Working with the theme of recycling, Walcott-Ayers used pencil to create a number of rough sketches of their ideas. They used the sketches as visual references while drawing on-screen.

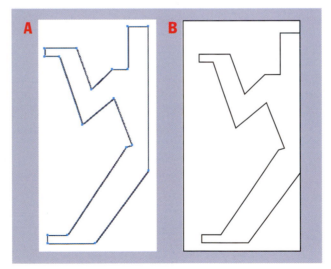

2 Drawing a figure and background

The center of the poster features a stylized human figure made of straight lines. It was created by clicking the pen tool from point to point to create half of the figure (A). A rectangle was drawn around the figure half, its right edge aligned to the right edge of the figure, using a black stroke and white fill for both elements (B).

3 Reflecting the figure

To create a symmetrical figure, the designers selected the figure half and rectangle and used the Copy and Paste In Front commands to create a clone. They selected the reflect tool, Option-clicked on the right edge of the graphic to set a reference point and to open the Reflect dialog box, and clicked the Vertical button to reflect the cloned elements across the vertical axis.

4 Adding Pantone color

To color the graphic with Pantone colors, the designers first chose Import Styles from the File menu and opened the Pantone Process Color System from the Color Systems folder to load the colors of this system into the Paint Style palette. They then selected the elements of the graphic and changed their line and fill to either yellow (PMS 115) or purple (PMS 2597).

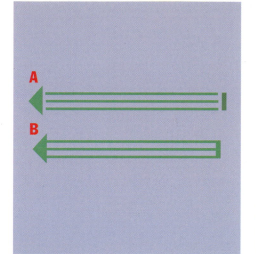

5 Creating an arrow

To create a stylized arrow Walcott-Ayers used the pen tool to draw a triangle, 3 horizontal lines 1.5-points thick, and a short vertical 2.7-point line (A) and assembled them to create the arrow (B).

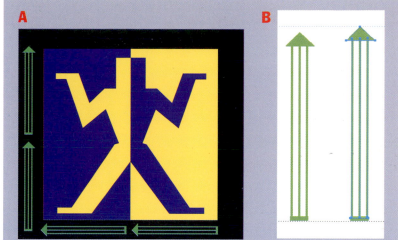

6 Positioning, rotating, and adjusting the arrows

The designers drew a black rectangle behind the figure graphic and positioned the arrow and a copy at the bottom so that their combined length matched the width of the graphic. They then copied and rotated the original arrow by 90 degrees, lengthened it slightly, and positioned it and a copy along the left edge of the black background (A). The original arrow was lengthened by dragging the pointer tool to select the points in the triangle and line ends and dragging them up (B).

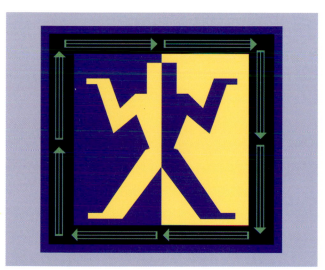

7 Completing the central design

The designers continued to copy, rotate, and adjust the length of the original arrows in 90-degree increments until they had created a pattern of 8 arrows around the figure graphic, which reinforced the conference theme of resource recycling.

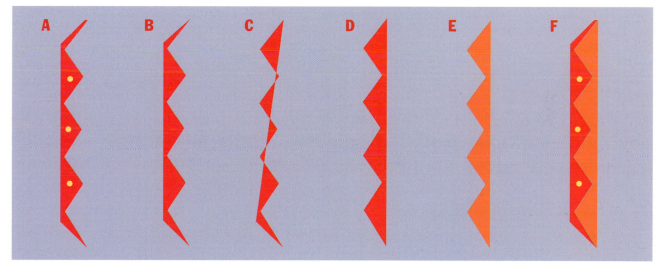

8 Creating an interlocked zigzag pattern

To create a colorful zigzag pattern, the designers used the pen tool to draw a zigzag shape, filled it with red, and added 3 small yellow circles (A). Then, to create an interlocking piece, they selected and copied the red shape and used the delete-anchor-point tool (from the scissors tool submenu) to click on and delete 1 of the points near the top to create a sharp corner (B). They then deleted the corner point at the upper left of the shape, which temporarily produced a twisted shape (C). They deleted the corner point at the bottom left of the shape, and the shape was automatically adjusted to create a new shape with a zigzag edge identical to that of the original and a straight edge along its right side (D). Walcott-Ayers filled this shape with orange (E) and positioned it next to the original (F).

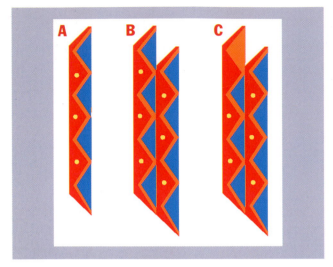

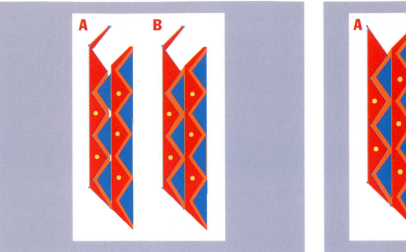

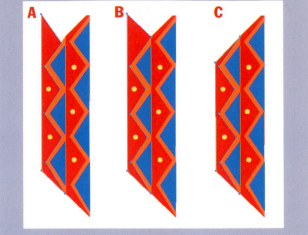

9 Completing the zigzag pattern

To complete the zigzag pattern the designers drew a blue triangle, made 3 copies, and positioned them along the right edge of the red and orange interlocked pattern (A). They then copied all the elements and positioned the copy next to the original so that their 2 bottom edges aligned on a diagonal line (B). They deleted the blue triangle and yellow circle at the top left (C).

10 Editing points of the orange shape

To make the top of the left-hand zigzag pattern align along a diagonal line with the original, as their bottom edges do, the delete-anchor-point tool was used to remove the top point of the left-hand orange shape (A), and then the direct-selection tool was used to select and move the orange shape's new top point to meet the top left corner of the adjacent red shape (B).

11 Editing points of the red shape

The delete-anchor-point tool was used to delete the top 2 points of the left-hand red shape (A) and then the shape's top right-hand point was selected and dragged to meet the top left-hand point of the red shape on the right (B). The top point of the left-hand red shape was selected and dragged down so that the shape's top line was on the same diagonal as its neighbor (C).

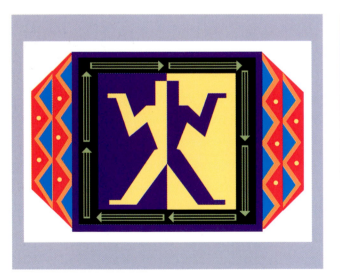

12 Copying and reflecting the zigzags

The finished zigzag pattern was positioned to the left of the central recycling graphic and then copied. The copy was flipped across the vertical axis with the -reflect tool and the reflected copy was positioned along the right edge of the central graphic to complete a symmetrical central element.

13 Drawing borders and a background

Following their sketches, the designers drew a black background rectangle, positioned the recycling graphic and zigzags at its center, and drew red diagonal lines with 90 degree corners to mask off the rough edges. A blue line was added around all the elements.

14 Creating a checkerboard pattern

To create a checkerboard pattern for the triangle below the recycling graphic, the designers used the rectangle tool with the Shift key held down to draw a small square, used Copy and Paste In Front to clone the square, and moved the clone to the right (A). They typed Command-C, -F, -D (Copy, Paste In Front, and Repeat Transform) to produce a row of 15 squares (B) and then copied the row and positioned the copy below the original (C).

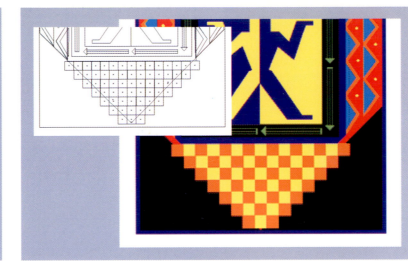

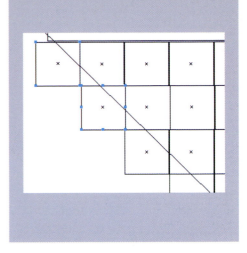

15 Coloring and assembling the checkerboard

The designers assigned colors to the fills and strokes of the 2 rows of squares, alternating between yellow and orange. They then copied the 2 rows and positioned rows below each other until they had produced a grid of 7 rows large enough to completely cover the triangular area they wanted to fill. They positioned the checkerboard over the poster design.

16 Deleting squares from the checkerboard

In Artwork mode, which showed the underlying objects, the unnecessary squares of the grid were deleted until the checkerboard elements were trimmed back to the shape of the triangle.

17 Editing the squares along the edges

To trim the orange squares along the border of the triangle shape, the designers selected them and chose Add Anchor Points from the Objects submenu from the Filter menu. This added a point in the middle of each side of the squares.

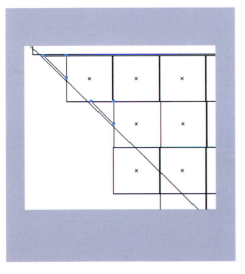

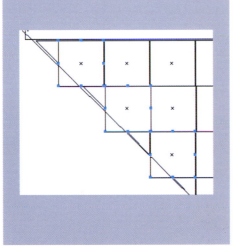

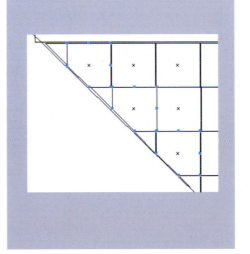

18 Deleting points from the orange squares

Then the delete-anchor-point tool was used to delete the points that overlapped the diagonal lines in the graphic, so that each of the squares was trimmed to a small triangle.

19 Adding points to the yellow squares

The Add Anchor Points filter was used again to add points to the yellow squares that overlapped the diagonal lines.

20 Deleting points from the yellow squares

The outside corner point of each yellow square was deleted so that the squares were trimmed back to a polygon shape that did not overlap the diagonal line along the border of the large triangle shape.

21 Finishing the checkerboard

When all the overlapping squares had been trimmed back, the designers used Bring To Front to position the red lines in front of the checkerboard to mask off the uneven edges of the edited squares.

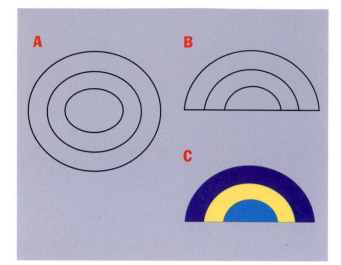

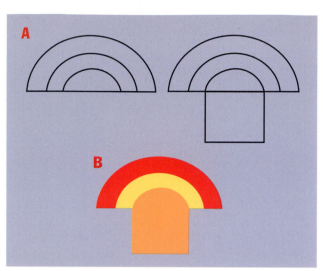

22 Creating a half-oval design
To create a pattern of overlapping rings for the top of the design, the designers first used the oval tool to draw an oval and then scaled 2 copies of it to create a pattern of 3 nested ovals (A). They then used the scissors tool to cut the ovals and deleted their unwanted bottom parts (B). They added color to the oval element (C).

23 Using the Unite filter
To fill gaps that might occur when the half-ovals were overlapped, the designers created an element with an extended bottom. A square was drawn below the inner half-oval (A), both elements were selected, the Unite command (under Pathfinder under Filters) was used to combine them into one path, and the new element was filled with color (B).

24 Copying and varying color
The designers made many copies of the 2 half-oval elements and varied the color combinations in them. They then arranged the elements in rows, shown here before they were overlapped.

25 Assembling and trimming the pattern
Ten rows of half-oval elements were layered over the triangular shape the designers wanted to fill, and then the unnecessary, overlapping edges of the half-ovals that fell along the diagonal lines of the triangle were cut away using the same techniques as for the checkerboard pattern.

26 Adding a poster frame and background
To complete the graphic elements of the poster, the designers positioned the layered half-oval pattern behind the red diagonal lines at the top of the recycling graphic, and then drew a large black rectangle background at the poster's finished size of 18 x 26 inches and used the pen tool to draw a rough-edged inner background shape filled with light yellow.

27 Creating type along a path
To create a decorative type element for the top of the poster, the designers drew 2 thick red arcs as borders and a thinner black arc to serve as a path for the type (A). They clicked on the arc with the path-type tool and entered the date in 17-point Gill Sans Bold, centered, with a track of 30/1000 em. The type flowed along the curve of the arc (B), which became invisible.

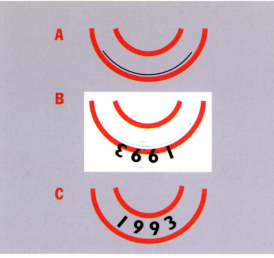

A

B

C

PUTTING RECYCLING TO WORK

PUTTING RECYCLING TO WORK

PUTTING RECYCLING TO WORK

28 Flipping type along a path

To create a type element for the poster bottom, the designers copied and flipped the 2 red arcs and drew a new black arc to serve as the type path (A). They centered numerals in 18.5-point Gill Sans Bold with a Horizontal Scale of 110% and a Track of 200/1000 em. The numerals appeared upside down (B) until the I-beam was dragged upward to flip them (C).

29 Setting and spacing headline type

To create a large headline for the bottom of the poster, the designers set type in Emigre's Senator Tall at 60 points (A). They increased the Horizontal Scale to 138% to make the characters wider (B) and then set the track at 15/1000 em to put more space between characters (C). The designers positioned the type on the poster and added more black type set in 12-point Gill Sans.

The finished poster design was printed both as a rolled poster on heavy stock (as shown in the opening illustration) and as a folded conference guide with the conference schedule printed on the back.

30 Creating a 2-color poster back

To create graphic elements for the 2-color back of the poster, the designers made 2 copies of the recycling graphic from the poster design and changed the color fills and strokes to make 2 new variations. A pastel version (A) is composed of a 30% tint of the yellow used in the original and a 20% tint of the purple. The second variation is composed of 100% purple, yellow, and white and does not include the arrows used in the original (B). The designers also created zigzag and checkerboard elements in yellow and purple, following the style of the front of the poster, and placed these around the border of the poster back along with the newly colored recycling logos, a yellow background, and purple headline type (C). They finished the poster back by adding 3 columns of body text describing the conference activities (D).

36

Splitting Long Paths

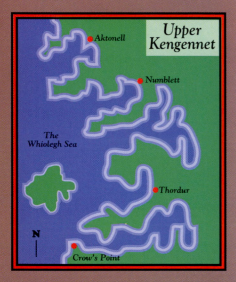

Long paths with many anchor points can sometimes present a problem in printing an illustration. You can reduce the time needed for output and eliminate "limitcheck" errors by splitting complex paths into smaller components that are easier for output devices to handle.

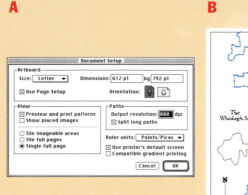

A

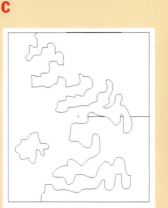

B

C   **D**

1 Splitting paths automatically

Illustrator's Document Setup function provides a Split Long Paths function that will automatically break up long, complex paths so that a file will be easier to output (A). The breaks are achieved by cutting the original path (B) into several segments and then closing each segment with a straight line to connect the cut ends (C). The divisions are invisible in the final illustration, so that the split object looks the same as it would without splitting (D).

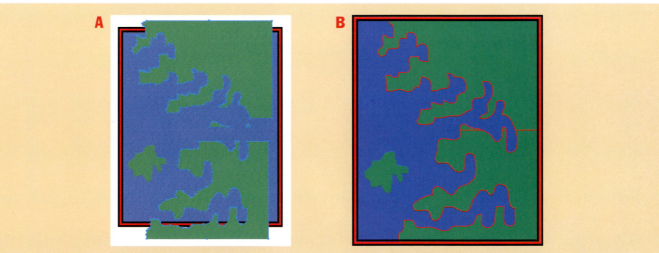

A   **B**

2 Understanding the limitations of Split Long Paths

In the default Document Setup the Split Long Paths function is turned off. This is because dividing complex objects into several unattached pieces is likely to make the file more difficult to edit than the original illustration, since moving, copying, or transforming the object would require identifying and selecting all of its several parts (A). Another limitation of Split Long Paths is that it doesn't work on paths that are stroked, because the split would put visible lines across the object (B). Nor does it work on masks or compound objects, since the split would ruin the compounding or masking effect.

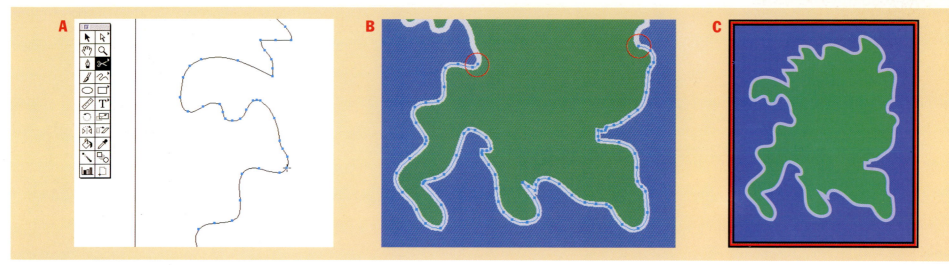

3 Splitting stroked paths

Although they can't be split automatically, stroked paths can be split successfully using the scissors tool (A). Cutting the path at 2 points divides it into 2 objects, with end points that exactly overlap at the point of cutting (B). The stroke and fill are divided, but since the 2 paths remain open, no unwanted new strokes are created. And the 2 new objects exactly abut, so that they still appear to be a single object (C).

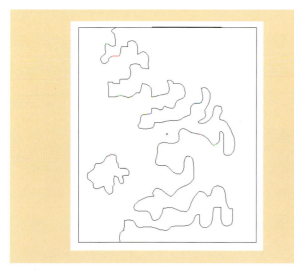

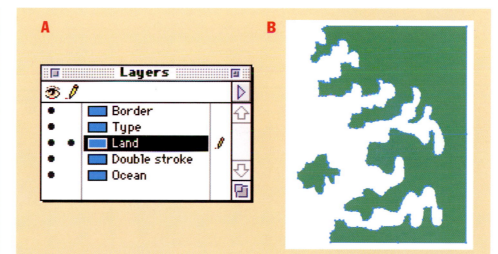

4 Rejoining split paths

If a path is split for output and then additional changes to that part of the illustration are needed, the paths can be rejoined to make it easier to edit the original object. Select all parts of the split object and apply the Pathfinder Unite filter. After editing, you can split the path again for printing.

5 Keeping track of split objects

Using the Unite filter (as described in step 4) requires selecting all parts of a split object so that they can be put back together. To make it easy to identify and select all the parts of an object you plan to split, use the Layers palette to create a separate layer for the object before you split it (A). Then, if you need to select all of its parts after splitting, you can lock all layers except the layer for that object (by turning off their pencil icons), select all the objects on that layer, and apply the Unite filter (B).

37

Trapping Artwork

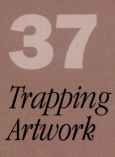

Autumn

That time of year thou mayst in me behold
When yellow leaves, or none, or few, do hang

If your Adobe Illustrator artwork will be color-separated
for printing, you may need to
provide trapping. The next 6
pages explain what trapping is
and how it can be achieved in
Illustrator. Ask your printer for
advice on whether and how
much to trap.

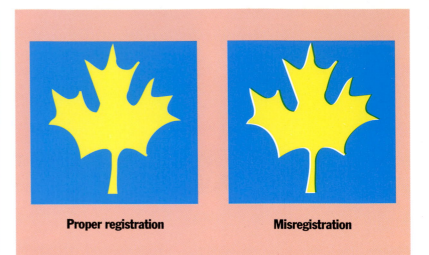

Proper registration   **Misregistration**

Knocking out

Adobe Illustrator builds artwork in layers. When an Illustrator document is
printed, colors in lower layers are typically knocked out so that the colors of
objects or type on upper layers can print clearly.

Understanding misregistration

When a document is printed, the paper can stretch or shift as the sheet moves through the press.
This can cause *misregistration* of the ink colors, and gaps can occur between colors so that the
unprinted paper of the knock-out shows through in places where it should instead be covered with
ink. (The effect is exaggerated here.) This can be distracting to the eye, diminishing the effect of
the artwork.

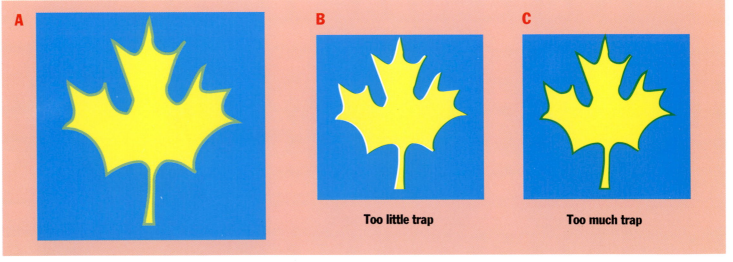

Too little trap   **Too much trap**

Preventing gaps

Trapping is the process of building slight overlaps between objects of different colors, so that stretching or shifts in any direction can occur without producing gaps. The overlap can be created by extending 1 color into the other
at the edge where the 2 colors meet. In effect, this overlap produces a band of
an intermediate color between the 2 original colors (A). With too little trap,

gaps can still occur (B). Too much trap produces an outline or border effect that can be almost as
distracting as a gap (C). The printer — that is, the person who will print the artwork — will
know best how much of an overlap will be required to prevent gaps between colors for any particular project. Trapping can be done as the artwork is produced in programs such as Illustrator.
Or it can be done later, when the film is being made; in that case the trapping may be done with
programs designed specifically for that purpose.

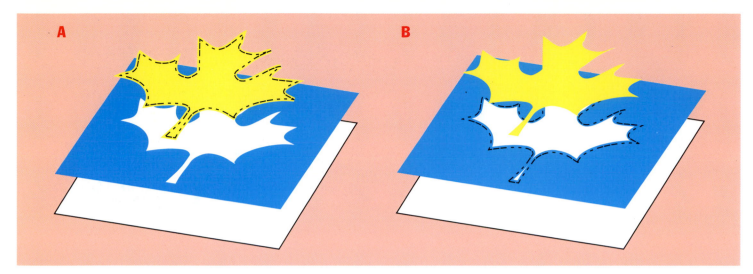

Trapping a shape

An object can be trapped either by enlarging the object slightly, called *spreading* (A) or by shrinking the knock-out a little, called *choking* (B). **Note:** All diagrams of trapping shown in this chapter are exaggerated to make it easier to see the point of the illustrations; in reality, trapping involves extremely narrow overlaps, typically fractions of a point. Other than the exaggerated traps in the diagrams, the art has no trap at all, except that black type is overprinted.

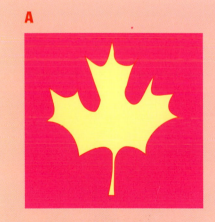

Choking with the dark color

Spreading with the dark color

Spreading with the light color

Choking with the light color

Deciding whether to spread or choke

The decision about whether to spread the object or choke the background depends on the 2 colors involved. Trapping with the darker color can produce unsuccessful results. Choking with the darker color can visibly shrink the object (A). Spreading with the darker color can cause perceptible thickening (B). Spreading (C) or choking (D) with the lighter color makes the trap less apparent and more closely maintains the original shape of the object.

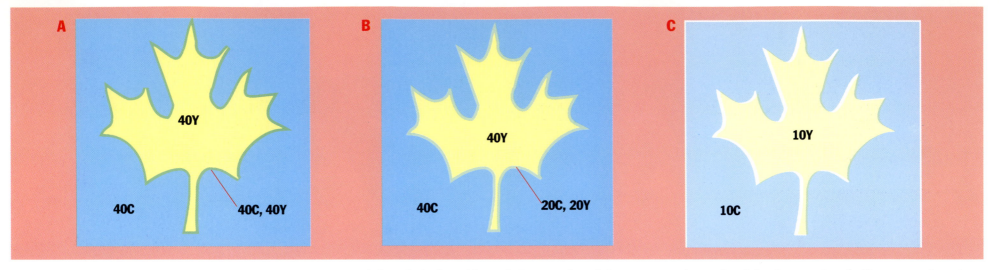

Trapping with a third color

Sometimes the color that forms from the overlap when trapping is added to a pale object on a pale background is markedly darker than either of the 2 original colors, producing an outline effect (A).

Instead of using both colors at full strength, the trap can be made from a lighter tint of the mix of the 2 colors (B) or a mix of a tint of 1 color with the other color at full strength.

In the case of very light colors, it may be preferable not to trap. That is, the small white gap that can appear if misregistration occurs (C) may be less obtrusive than the "border" effect that can happen when trap is added. ● *Ask your printer for advice about trapping very light colors and about other unusual trapping situations.*

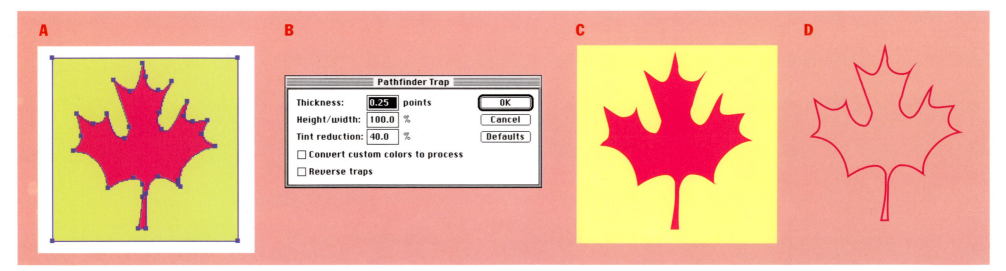

Trapping filled shapes automatically

Illustrator 5.5 includes a filter specifically designed for trapping. To apply the Pathfinder Trap filter, select the filled, no-stroke object and background you want to trap (A) and choose Trap from the Pathfinder submenu of the Filter menu. The amount of trap is specified in the Pathfinder Trap dialog box; enter the exact trap Thickness requested by your printer (B). When you click

OK, Illustrator automatically analyzes the colors and creates an object that spreads or chokes a tint of the lighter color into the darker (C, D). (By default, the color of the overlap area is a mix of 100% of the darker color and 40% of the lighter color.) Illustrator's determination of the color for the trap is based on a mathematical analysis of the composition of the colors involved. This analysis might produce a different color than you would choose

based on a visual examination. If you want to change the trap color based on what you see on-screen, the Pathfinder Trap dialog box gives you 2 ways to do it. You can increase or decrease the contribution from the lighter color by changing the Tint Reduction. Or select Reverse Trap to use the "lighter" color at full strength and to apply the Tint Reduction to the "darker" color.

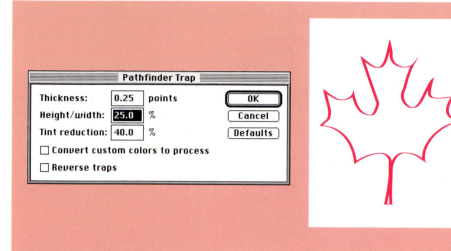

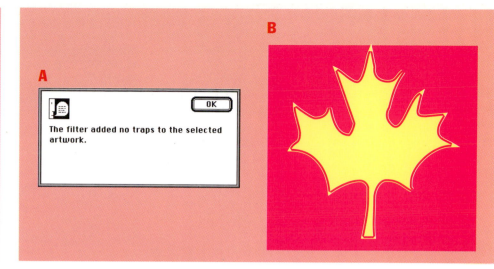

Varying the trap thickness

The Height/Width setting lets you apply different amounts of trap on vertical than on horizontal elements, in case the printing process is likely to cause misregistration in 1 direction more than the other. Set the trap Thickness that your printer requests for trapping vertical lines. Then change the Height/Width ratio to put more (up to 400%) or less (as little as 25%) trap on horizontal elements.

Applying the Trap filter inappropriately

Illustrator's Trap filter works correctly with filled, no-stroke objects. It does not work with type or with strokes. Also, if no trap is necessary because the object and background share common color components, or if only 1 object has been selected, no trap will be created.; a dialog box will notify you that no trap has been made (A). If you apply the Trap filter to a stroked-and-filled object, the trap will be created, but the result will be wrong. The trapping band of color will be made at the edge of the fill, not at the outer edge of the stroke; resulting in a thin strip of color set in from the edge of the object (B).

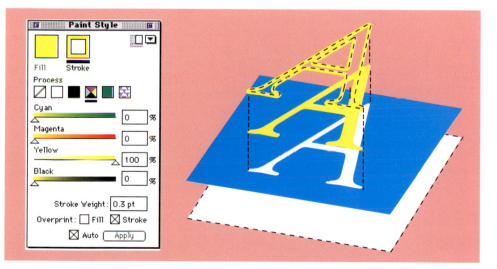

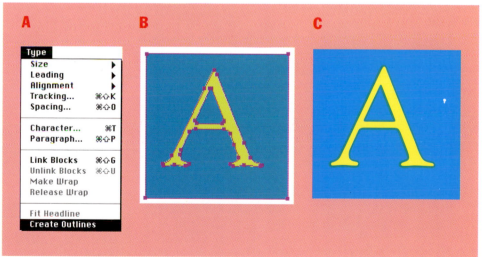

Trapping display type

The decision about whether to choke or spread can be especially important for trapping type, because of its fine strokes and details. Type can be trapped by designating a color for an overprinted stroke in the Paint Style dialog box. ● *While large colored display type can be trapped successfully, small colored type is difficult to trap successfully by spreading or choking because the thickness of the trap can be quite large relative to the thickness of the type.*

Trapping type automatically

Although the Pathfinder Trap filter does not work on type, you can use it to trap large type by first converting the type to objects. Set the type and then choose Create Outlines from the Type menu. Then select the converted type (A) and its background (B) and apply the Trap filter to make the trap (C).

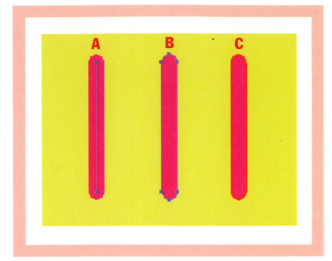

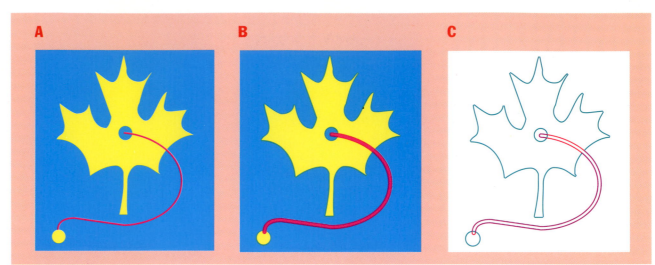

Trapping a line

The Pathfinder Trap filter does not work on lines that are created as unfilled strokes. But you can trap a line by first converting it to a filled object and then applying the Trap filter. Draw the line (A), select it, and apply the Outline Path filter to turn it into a filled, no-stroke object (B). Then select the new object and its background and apply the Trap filter (C).

Trapping complex artwork

The Pathfinder Trap filter can create trap for an object that crosses several different background colors. Select the object and its background objects (in this case we selected the magenta line, which had been converted to outlines, the yellow leaf, the cyan background rectangle and the two small circles) (A). Apply the Trap filter to create trap (B). (The 2 small circles were trapped

against their respective backgrounds in an earlier trapping operation.) Note that the trap changes color as it crosses from 1 background color to another (C). If part of the trapped object extends onto a white background, no trap is created (because none is needed) where the object falls on white.

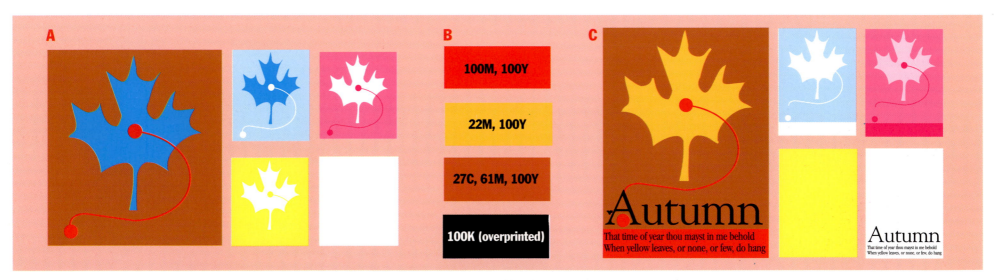

Avoiding the need for trapping process colors

For an illustration prepared with process printing colors (cyan, magenta, yellow, and black), color separation results in a printing plate for each of these primary colors (A). These plates are used to apply the inks. One way to avoid the potential for white gaps due to misregistration is to make sure that every color you use in an illustration shares at least one primary color component

with every other color in the illustration (B). That way, when separations are made, there is no potential for white gaps (C). If misregistration occurs when the illustration is printed, a sliver of the shared color will show, but this is usually much less distracting than white would be. Ask your printer for advice on the percentage of shared color needed to avoid trapping.

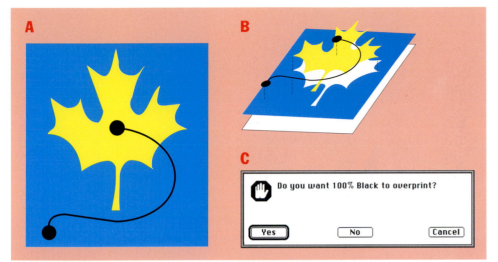

Overprinting black

Since black is dark enough to cover other colors, it can be trapped by overprinting it (A, B). The overprinting can be set up on an object-by-object basis in the Paint Style palette (see "Trapping display type" on page 129), or by designating 100% black ink to overprint in all cases through Adobe Separator (C). ⚫ *Versions 5 and later of Adobe Illustrator do not automatically overprint black. This color, like all others, must be set to overprint if you want it to do so.*

Trapping color against black

When you want to trap a colored object or type against a black background, you can add the color to the black. This is equivalent to adding a layer (or layers) of color under the black (A). It not only provides trap but also makes the black richer, as you can see by comparing the 3 black swatches shown here (B). Check with your printer to make sure that this procedure won't result in a total ink coverage that's too high to print well. If necessary, reduce the percentage of color in the black.

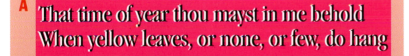

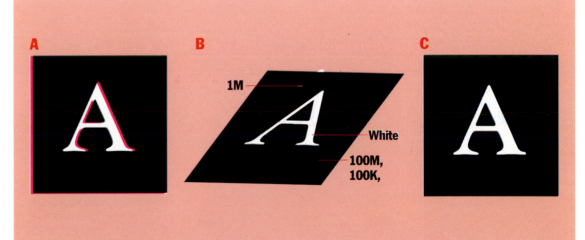

Trapping text

Knocking out black text type from a colored background is risky because slight misregistration can make the type hard to read (A). For black text, overprinting the type is a good way of avoiding misregistration gaps without thickening or thinning the strokes of the letters by using a trapping stroke (B). For type in color on a black background, add the color to the black (C) as described in "Trapping color against black" (above right).

Trapping white on an "enriched" black background

When an object or type is reversed out of an "enriched" black background, misregistration can cause a "halo" of color at the edge of the white (A). To prevent this, overprint a "process white" stroke: Define the stroke's color as 1% of each process primary that has been added to the black, and set the stroke to overprint (B). This small amount of color will not show in the white type or object, but it will "push" color back from the edges, leaving only solid black, to provide a crisp outline (C).

How This Book Was Produced

This book was assembled in Aldus PageMaker 4.2, using illustrations created in Adobe Illustrator 5.5 and earlier versions.

1 Placing the artwork

Finished Adobe Illustrator artwork for each chapter, as well as some of the step-by-step figures, was saved in EPS format, with Color Macintosh selected in the Save As dialog box so that an EPSF header and a color PICT version of the artwork would be saved along with the file. The EPSF header allowed the artwork to be placed and printed from the PageMaker file; the PICT provided an on-screen preview so we could see the artwork as it would appear on the page.

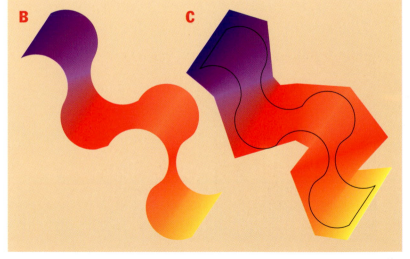

2 Showing progressive steps

To show the steps used to create each piece of finished artwork, we opened the file in Adobe Illustrator 5.5, edited the artwork to show each intermediate step we wanted, and used Save As to save the new, altered copies of the file as EPS's. We often made the last illustrations in a series first, since they required the least editing, and then we progressively removed elements from the artwork to make the earlier steps (A).

To see how complex elements had been constructed, we could select an element and then check to see whether Release was available as an option under Masks or under Compound Paths in the Object menu. If so, we released the mask or compound to see how the complex object had been put together. In this example, releasing the mask on a curving shape (B) reveals the blends that have been masked into it (C).

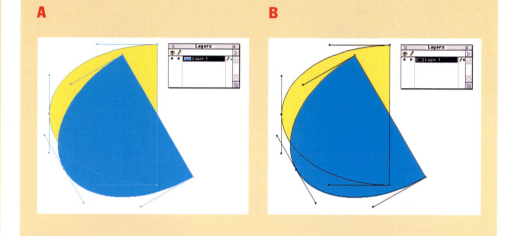

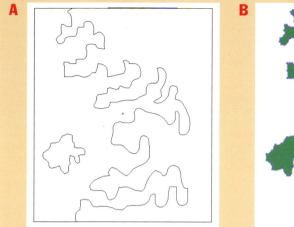

3 Making screen shots

When it was important to show the construction details of some stage of the artwork, we made screen captures by using System 7's built-in screen-capture function (Command-Shift-3) or by using Screenshot, a program dedicated to that task. Some screen captures were made from files in Artwork view (A); others were made in Preview mode (B). Screen captures were automatically saved in PICT format; we then used Adobe Photoshop to convert them to TIFF format so they could be placed in the PageMaker files and separated with Aldus PrePrint.

4 Changing the highlight color

For many of the screen shots, Illustrator 5.5's default blue highlight color was used for showing paths, anchor points, and direction lines (A). But in some cases the highlight color was changed through the Layer Options dialog box, opened by choosing Layer Options in the Layers palette (B). *Choosing a highlight color that contrasts with the surrounding strokes and fills makes it easier to construct and adjust paths.*

5 Hiding page details

Illustrator shows an outline of the current page in its working window (A). If we wanted to take a screen shot of the artwork without showing its relationship to the entire page, we could make the page outline invisible by choosing Hide Page Tiling from the View menu (B).

6 Establishing and saving views

To zero in on a part of the artwork that we wanted to show in a screen shot, we clicked on it with the magnifying glass tool, zooming into (enlarging) that area in steps that doubled its magnification until we had the view we wanted. To zoom out, we Option-clicked with the same tool. If we wanted to enlarge our view of a particular area of the artwork as much as possible, we dragged diagonally across the desired area with the magnifying tool (A), and the area was enlarged to fill the window (B). So that we could return to the same view again if we wanted to alter it slightly and make another screen shot, we saved our views by choosing New View from the view menu, naming this custom view, and clicking OK (C); we could open them again by selecting the named view from the list at the bottom of the View menu.

Contributing Artists

Mary Adsit
3557 Keating Street
San Diego, CA 92110
619/542-0513

CWA, Inc.
Calvin Woo and Susan Merritt
4015 Ibis
San Diego, CA 92103
619/299-0431, 299-0451 fax

Jack Davis and Jill Davis
JHDavis Design
Encinitas, CA

EuroStyle Advertising Inc.
Ursula Sattler-Cohen, Claudia
Braunwarth, Michele Davison
740 13th Street, Suite 502
San Diego, CA 92101
619/238-0854, 238-0726 fax

Lance Hidy Associates
10 State Street
Newburyport, MA 01950
508/465-1346, 465-8632 fax

Matsuri Graphics
P.O. Box 6926
Bloomington, IN 47407
812/336-1326, 339-5422 fax

Jim McConlogue
Warner Design Associates
3920 Conde Street
San Diego, CA 92110
619/297-4455, 297-2610 fax

Steve McGuire
60 Alhambra Hills Drive
Martinez, CA 94553
510/228-6096

Steve Musgrave
202 S. State, #1324
Chicago, IL 60604
312/939-4717, 939-4718 fax

John Odam
John Odam Design Associates
2163 Cordero Road
Del Mar, CA 92014
619/259-8230, 259-8469 fax

Daniel Pelavin
90 Varick Street, Suite 3B
New York, NY 10013
212/941-7418, 431-7138 fax

David Smith

Scott Summers
3820 22nd Street
San Francisco, CA 94114
415/821-1958

Jim Walcott-Ayers and Liz Pollina
Walcott-Ayers Group
Trowbridge House
1230 Preservation Park
Oakland, CA 94612
510/444-5204, 444-2688 fax

Lin Wilson
1258 W. Cornelia Avenue, #1
Chicago, IL 60657
312/275-7172, 404-0117 fax

YO
Maria Giudice and Lynn Stiles
852 Folsom Street
San Francisco, CA 94107
415/357-4880, 357-4884 fax

Definitions

A listing of acronyms used in this book, what they stand for, and what they mean

DCS (Desktop Color Separation)
A specialized EPS (see below) file format that uses 5 components — 1 each for the cyan, magenta, yellow, and black color separation plates — and 1 composite image for screen display and low-resolution printing

EPS or **EPSF** (Encapsulated PostScript Format)
A PostScript language file that includes a PICT component (see below) so an image can be displayed on screen and the file can be printed from a non-PostScript printer

PS (PostScript)
The page description language that PageMaker and other desktop graphics programs use to generate instructions for output of graphics files

PICT/PICT2
A standard Macintosh format for black-and-white and color graphics

TIFF (Tagged Image File Format)
A file format used for scanned images and other bitmapped graphics

Resources

Adobe Illustrator, Adobe Streamline, Adobe Photoshop, and **Adobe typefaces** are available in the United States from
Adobe Systems Incorporated
1585 Charleston Road
Mountain View, CA 94039-7900
415/961-4400

in Europe from
Adobe Systems Europe B.V.
Europlaza, Hoogoorddreff 54a
1101 BE Amsterdam Z-O
The Netherlands

and in Japan from
Adobe Systems Japan
Ebisu Garden Place Tower
4-20-3, Ebisu, Shibuya-ku
Tokyo 150
Japan

Art Nouveau Images clip art
is available from
Silicon Designs
P.O. Box 2234
Orinda, CA 94563
USA
510/254-1460

ClickArt EPS Illustrations
clip art
is available from
T/Maker Company
1390 Villa Street
Mountain View, CA 94041
USA
415/962-0195

Designer's Club clip art
is available from
Dynamic Graphics
6000 N. Forest Park Drive
Peoria, IL 61614-3592
USA
800/255-8800

Emigre typefaces
are available from
Emigre Graphics
4475 D Street
Sacramento, CA 95819
USA
916/451-4344

Images with Impact clip art
is available from
3G Graphics
114 Second Avenue S. Suite 104
Edmonds, WA 98020
USA
206/774-3518

JapanClips clip art
is available from
Matsuri Graphics
P.O. Box 6926
Bloomington, IN 47407
812-336-1326, 812-339-5422 fax
USA

OPTIFonts typefaces
are available from
Eagle Graphic Systems
1824 Lakeshore Court
Fort Collins, CO 80525
USA
303-226-4567

The Pictorial Archive series of
printed clip art is available from
Dover Publications
31 East Second Street
Mineola, NY 11501
USA

Screenshot
is available from
Baseline Publishing, Inc.
1770 Moriah Woods Blvd., Suite 14
Memphis, TN 38117
USA
901/682-9676

Index

About the Authors

Janet Ashford is a writer and artist focusing on computer illustration and design. She is a regular contributor to *MacUser*, *Print,* and *Step-By-Step Graphics* magazines and is a contributing editor of *Step-By-Step Electronic Design* newsletter. She is coauthor of the *Verbum Book of PostScript Illustration* and contributed illustrations to the *Verbum Book of Digital Painting*, *The Desktop Color Book,* and *The Photo CD Book*. She created interface screens and composed original music for a Photo CD disk accompanying *The Official Photo CD Handbook.* She is co-author with Linnea Dayton of *Aldus PageMaker: A Visual Guide for the Mac.* Ashford's background in traditional fine art media and music combined with her experience as a computer illustrator and designer gives her a special understanding of the computer graphics and multimedia fields. Ashford is also the author of *The Whole Birth Catalog*, *Birth Stories: The Experience Remembered*, *Mothers & Midwives: A History of Traditional Childbirth*, and for nine years edited and published *Childbirth Alternatives Quarterly*. Her three children were born at home. A violinist since the age of nine, Ashford plays with a traditional string band, Lime in the Harp. She lives in Solana Beach, California.

Linnea Dayton is a contributing editor for and former editor-in-chief of *Step-By-Step Electronic Design*, a full-color monthly newsletter for graphic designers and illustrators using the computer. She is also a contributing editor for *Step-By-Step Graphics* magazine. Formerly managing editor of *Verbum* magazine, she is coauthor of the Verbum Book series (*PostScript Illustration*, *Electronic Page Design*, *Digital Painting*, *Scanned Imagery,* and *Digital Typography*) as well as *The Desktop Color Book, The Photo CD Book,* and *The Photoshop Wow! Book*. Dayton has also written an interactive column for *Verbum Interactive,* a magazine on CD-ROM, and is interested in exploring the medium of interactive fiction. Among other accomplishments she remembers with fondness and pride are starting a thriving alternative class in the public school system, backpacking more than 150 miles in the mountains of Nepal, and fledging two offspring. She lives in Solana Beach, California.